THE
APOCALYPTIC
MOVEMENT
INTRODUCTION &
INTERPRETATION

WALTER SCHMITHALS
TRANSLATED BY JOHN E. STEELY

ABINGDON PRESS

Nashville   New York

DIE APOKALYPTIK: EINFÜHRUNG UND DEUTUNG
Copyright © 1973 by Vandenhoeck & Ruprecht, Göttingen
THE APOCALYPTIC MOVEMENT: INTRODUCTION AND
INTERPRETATION
Translation copyright © 1975 by Abingdon Press
All rights reserved.

Library of Congress Cataloging in Publication Data

Schmithals, Walter.
 The apocalyptic movement, introduction and interpretation.
 Translation of Die Apokalyptik.
 Bibliography: p.
 1. Apocalyptic literature. I. Title.
BS646.S3413   273'.1   74-34242

ISBN 0-687-01630-4

*Acknowledgment is made to the following publishers for permission to
use copyright material:*
Association Press, for material from *The Relevance of Apocalyptic* by
H. H. Rowley.
Basil Blackwell for material from *Theocracy and Eschatology* by Otto
Plöger.
Fortress Press for material from *New Testament Questions of Today*
by Ernst Käsemann.
Christian Kaiser Verlag for permission to translate from *Theologie des
Alten Testaments* by Gerhard von Rad (4th German ed.).
Verlag W. Kohlhammer for permission to translate material from
Ecclesia Spiritualis by Ernst Benz, "Der revolutionäre Geist" by Leszek
Kolakowski, and *Jahweglaube and Zukunftserwartung* by H. D.
Preuss.
Lutterworth Press for material from *The Kingdom of God and the Son
of Man* by Rudolf Otto.
Oliver and Boyd for material from *Old Testament Theology* by Gerhard
von Rad.
The Clarendon Press for material from *Epistle to the Romans* by Karl
Barth, trans. E. C. Hoskyns, 1933; and *Apocrypha and Pseudepig-
rapha of the Old Testament*, edited by R. H. Charles, Vol. 2, 1913.
Reprinted by permission of The Clarendon Press, Oxford.
The Westminster Press for material from *New Testament Apocrypha*,
Volume Two, edited by Wilhelm Schneemelcher and Edgar Hennecke.
English translation edited by R. McL. Wilson. Published in the U.S.A.
by The Westminster Press, 1963. Copyright © 1959, J. C. B. Mohr
(Paul Siebeck), Tübingen. English translation © 1963, Lutterworth
Press. Used by permission.

MANUFACTURED BY THE PARTHENON PRESS AT
NASHVILLE, TENNESSEE, UNITED STATES OF AMERICA

CONTENTS

TRANSLATOR'S PREFACE

Professor Schmithals' books in the field of New Testament are being cited with increasing frequency by his colleagues throughout the world. This recognition is an indication of the importance of his work and of the stimulation which it provides for the discussion of significant issues and problems. It is a pleasure, therefore, to have a share in bringing the present work to the attention of the English-reading public. Though it is addressed to a wider public than the author's earlier books, it should prove valuable to the specialists in the field as well, and particularly to students of the background and beginnings of Christianity.

I should like to express my gratitude to Professor Schmithals for his generous encouragement and his gracious response to my inquiries; to the Reverend W. W. Finlator for his unfeigned interest and support; to my students who let me share with them my enthusiasm for this undertaking; and to my family, who have had a part in the labor and the satisfaction involved in translating this book.

John E. Steely
Wake Forest, North Carolina
June 12, 1974

FOREWORD

The subject of apocalyptic comes up frequently in theological discussions nowadays, for its legacy continues to be a lively one. But it is also found in post-Christian world views; apparently there are elements in apocalyptic which can dispense with the religious garments.

Not everyone consciously lives on the legacy of apocalyptic, and often someone who appeals to this heritage knows too little about apocalyptic to be justified in making his appeal to it.

In any case, therefore, it will be profitable to concern ourselves with an examination of apocalyptic. The eleven chapters in this book, each one complete in itself, are addressed, with what I hope is recognizably current topical interest, to the historical phenomenon of apocalyptic. They are based on a series of lectures which were delivered before a group of seriously interested but not technically trained people. Hence they avoid all unnecessary scholarly apparatus and can be understood by people who are not specialists in the field.

Of course, the attention of specialists is welcomed also; for the investigation of and acquaintance with apocalyptic has not yet reached the point where an introduction to its problems cannot uncover new aspects and serve the discussion at the scholarly level.

Undoubtedly the perspective from which the phenomenon of apocalyptic is viewed in the present work is not the only one possible, but it is a necessary and, I hope, a fruitful one, with respect both to apocalyptic itself and to our present time. This study takes as its point of departure the position that the apocalyptic conceptions and ideas, considered in context, are an expression of a specific understanding of existence which can also be expressed in nonapocalyptic ways and which appears in manifold forms down to the present day. We shall try to understand apocalyptic in this sense as a unitary phenomenon. In this, different studies about the place in history of individual apocalyptic writings, about developments within the apocalyptic thought-world, and about historically conditioned distinctions within apocalyptic thought are not meant to be hindered, but rather encouraged. For understanding apocalyptic, the way from the specific to the general is equally as important as that from the general to the specific.

We shall make the totality of the apocalyptic understanding of existence the key to our preoccupation with apocalyptic, which best discloses its pertinence and present import in this way. In order to arrive at such information, to be sure, the whole of the present work must be taken into account. The reader who limits himself to the closing pages would not catch sight of the pertinence of our topic.

This pertinence discloses itself best to the person who

does not close his eyes to the fact that the intellectual and spiritual crisis of our time, regardless of how it may have been set in motion in detail, is rooted in the doubt whether there is any *meaning in history at all*. The apocalyptists, affected by the same crisis, give radical expression to this doubt, because they offer a way out of the crisis which in secularized form holds an absorbing interest for many people today.

THE THOUGHT-WORLD
OF APOCALYPTIC

The term "apocalyptic" comes from the Greek language and means "revelation." Nowadays it is used primarily to denote a religious movement in which "revelation" plays a special role, a movement within so-called late Judaism. This Judaism, whose religious documents in general were not accepted into the Hebrew canon of the Old Testament, is to be placed in the period from the third century B.C. down to New Testament times. In "apocalyptic" in this sense we are dealing with a widespread and significant movement, though not the only movement in late Judaism.

About the—fluctuating—number of believers in apocalyptic no firm statement can be made. On the whole, the saying of Jesus may very well apply to them: "Fear not, little flock; for it is your Father's good pleasure to give you the kingdom" (Luke 12:32). The apocalyptic movement had its center in Palestine, but its occasionally significant influence can be demonstrated in the Diaspora also.

The Apocalyptic Movement

To what extent there were also apocalyptic currents in other areas before, alongside, and after this Jewish apocalyptic will be treated at the appropriate place; at that time we shall also pose the question as to possible forerunners and prototypes as well as resultant later phenomena of Jewish apocalyptic. But it is undoubtedly true that every religious current which may be called "apocalyptic" acquires this designation by a comparison with Jewish apocalyptic, which, by virtue of the scope of its literary traditions, and of its influence extending down to the present, is the norm for the essence of what is apocalyptic.

Therefore this Jewish apocalyptic deserves our attention, which will be concerned more with its effects, seen as a whole, than with its origins. But above all we must explain its own peculiar character and bring that character into focus by comparing it with other religious movements.

First of all, however, we shall pose the relatively salient question how the apocalyptic world of concepts and ideas is presented to us in its "classical" form, which it acquired about two thousand years ago.

The main concern in apocalyptic is a set of truths which are not generally accessible and do not at once result from the rational consideration of reality, but must be revealed to man, must be announced to him from beyond himself. What the apocalyptist has to say is therefore new to his hearers; the one truth, formerly unknown but now revealed.

The authors of the apocalyptic writings were fully aware of the novelty of their ideas. Yet it was not their intention to form any new religious community. They were Jews, and their ideas were meant to be the expression of correct Jewish belief. But how could the new apocalyptic thought-material be connected with the Old Testament and Jewish tradition? During the same period Hellenistic Jews such as Philo of Alexandria were allegorizing the Old Testament in order to be able to keep it as the foundation of their teaching. Meanwhile, the apocalyptists helped themselves by placing their revelatory writings under the authority of one of the great figures of the Old Testament tradition. Enoch, Moses, Daniel, Ezra, Isaiah, and other recognized teachers of Israel are given as authors of apocalyptic revelatory writings. Their books are said to have remained hidden for a long time, in accordance with God's decree, sealed up from the eyes of the earlier generations. But now they are revealed, since the fulfillment of what was once written down in them by way of revelation is approaching and the generation has come for which they were written:

> For you Paradise is opened, the tree of life is planted;
> The future age made ready, blessedness prepared;
> The city built, a resting-place appointed;
> Good works created, wisdom prepared;
> The [evil] roots sealed off from you, illness eradicated
> before you;
> Death hidden, Hades put to flight;
> Corruption forgotten, sorrow passed away;
> But the treasures of immortality are revealed to you in
> the end.[1]

Accordingly, apocalyptic literature is not anonymous; the various individual works always name an author. It is pseudonymous; for undoubtedly none of the apocalyptic writings has any justification for the author's name which it bears.

By using these names, the authors of these writings achieved several things:

In the first place, in spite of their novelty their ideas received a stamp of authority from bearing the names of Judaism's recognized emissaries from God. Anyone who clung to these ideas and disseminated them could not be suspected of heresy. Indeed, anyone who accused them set himself, in so doing, in opposition to true Judaism.

Secondly, in this way people offered the proof of antiquity for the truth of the apocalyptic insights; this proof was highly regarded in ancient times, not least in the Judaism of that time. The Jews were always glad to point out to the Greeks that Moses had lived and written long before Homer and Plato and could rightly make a correspondingly higher claim to consideration than these Greek authorities.

But finally, by the early dating of their own writings people were able to incorporate into these an abundance of "vaticinia ex eventu"—predictions which were constructed after the fact, from past or contemporary history, and evoked in the reader the assurance that the revelations about what was to come deserved his full confidence. Hence it was not uncommon for the apocalypses to contain a comprehensive survey of history from the time of the purported author down to that of the actual author, whose identity is unknown to us; this survey guarantees the reliability of the apocalyptic information which followed it about the outcome of history.

For us these "vaticinia" have the rather considerable significance of making possible a more or less precise dating of the respective writings. For example, an apocalyptic book in which predictions about Nero are given could hardly have been written before the reign of Nero.

The Thought-World of Apocalyptic

The Book of Daniel, the only apocalypse to be accepted into the Hebrew canon of the Old Testament, can even be precisely dated with the aid of a "vaticinium ex eventu." The author, who has only a fairly deficient acquaintance with earlier history, shows himself to be increasingly well informed the closer he comes to his own time. He knows in detail the events of the year 168 B.C., when the Syrian king Antiochus IV, Epiphanes, on the return march from his unsuccessful campaign in Egypt vented his anger on the Jews and erected an altar to the Olympian Zeus on the altar of burnt offering in the temple at Jerusalem.[2] He knows of the revolt of the Maccabees that was set in motion by this act, and he knows that in December, 165, the temple could be rededicated. On the other hand, his description of the death of Antiochus, which came at the end of 164, is quite different from the way it actually happened. Thus one can with relative certainty date the Book of Daniel at the beginning of the year 164 B.C.

Of course, the apocalyptist's concern was not to relate past history with the help of "vaticinia ex eventu," particularly since these were all taken from familiar writings, but to give credibility to the predictions which referred to the future. For apocalyptic, revelation was in essence a revelation—apocalypsis—of an event in the future, even though it might be the immediate future.

However, the future occurrence did not stand alongside the past without any connection; for—and here we encounter a basic characteristic of apocalyptic—to the apocalyptist history is presented as a continuity which can be viewed as a whole, is complete, and is moving toward a goal. This insight once again, and presumably in a decisive way, explains the interest of the apocalyptist in having his books appear as documents from ancient times. It is true that in this way a large part of the *whole* of history, whose imminent consummation the apocalyptist is revealing, is presented to the reader in a unitary perspective, so that he can determine *his own place in the course of history* and, by understanding the future in terms of the past, and from its perspective, can properly relate himself to what is to come.

Thus the interest of the apocalyptist is directed to history not to the cosmos, in which the Greek of his time was interested, and indeed to history in its surveyable entirety. *To him* it is given to survey history as a whole; for he, the apocalyptist, knows about the goal, the end, of the ages, the consummation of history. Even that portion of history that has not yet happened has been revealed to him. So he already stands, even now, proleptically at the end of history, can survey it *entire*, and in the light of future events can also understand the past, interpret it, and make it comprehensible as a necessary step toward the established goal of the ages.

Therefore he also knows that the world's course is predetermined. One can know the future of the world, comprehend the past as necessary, and grasp the meaning of the totality of history, only if history is following an established plan. But the apocalyptist has no doubt on that point. God has previously fixed the world's course, and history is unfolding according to his eternal plan in orderly fashion, immune to outside influences. Just as for the Greek each thing has its fixed place in the cosmos, for the apocalyptist everything has its definite time in history, and anyone who knows the whole is able to understand the otherwise incomprehensible part.

Thus the apocalyptist understands history *by analogy* with the Greek cosmos. This also explains the cosmological elements in apocalyptic literature, in which it is set forth how God has precisely established the course of the stars, the times for light and darkness, the changing length of days, the rhythm of the moon's phases, and so forth; the unchangeability of the cosmic laws given by God provides for an understanding of the corresponding deterministic character of world history, and the insight of the apocalyptist, who on his celestial journeys looked behind the curtains of nature, into the precision of the cosmic processes, secured also for his view of history, the precision of which was really of concern to him, the necessary credibility and power of persuasion.[3]

Such a comprehensive view of history as is found in apocalyptic cannot very well understand history only as the history of a single nation. It must, in distinction from the Old Testament, keep in view the history of the world and of all nations and in fact apocalyptic even thinks in terms of universal history. For Jewish apocalyptic, of course, it is beyond question that in the history of the world of nations the fate of the people of Israel holds a special significance. But Israel's history is regarded as an outstanding portion of *world* history, not as the real history in whose sphere individual elements appear from the rest of the world's occurrences. Israel's way lies embedded in the totality of history, and only by the world's being historically brought to consummation is the way of Israel in the world also completed. It is not Israel that is judged, but the judgment of the world is imminent.

This universalistic thinking, which no longer exhibits a

primary interest in the fate of one nation, is matched by the process of individualization that can be observed in apocalyptic. When the world reaches its goal, then the individual man finds himself at this goal. It is not the salvation or doom of nations but the salvation or doom of humanity as the sum total of individual persons that moves the apocalyptist. The final destiny of the world interests him in the light of the final destiny of the individual; judgment and grace affect not societies, but the individual man, placing him in the "massa perditionis" or in the host of the elect righteous ones. The great contrast is not between Israel and the Gentiles, but between the godly and the ungodly. In all that happens, individual people are on their way, whether on the broad road of death, or on the narrow path of life. Books are kept in heaven on every individual man, and these are opened at the end of time. His good and evil works are weighed against each other in the scales, and each individual receives his sentence, the judgment of life unto life, or of death unto death.

In 4 Esdras 7:50 (cf. 8:1) we read: "The Most High has made not one age, but two"—a basic principle of apocalyptic thinking. Of these two ages, people know from experience only *this* age, the present, the old, the visible course of the world. It is full of trouble and woe, filled with perils and distresses. It is marked by sorrows and tears. Death rules in it. Discord and injustice fill it. It is called the "age of woes."[4]

Must we not expect that this course of the world will go on and on, that pain and misery will continue to determine the fate of men, even though their force will fluctuate? Will not death continue to rule? Or can one hope that the course of this world is getting better and is hastening toward a golden age? Such a hope is impossible! On the contrary, experience teaches us that it is getting worse and worse. The apocalyptist meets this present age with radical pessimism. The world is on a downward course and cannot be halted.

But one does not allow oneself to be cast down by this awareness. The apocalyptist also brings the new, unprecedented message that God has created not only this age, but also another one: a great age which is still hidden and invisible, but which has already been revealed to the apocalyptist. "God has established two kingdoms and created two ages, and has decreed that the present cosmos, which is unimportant and is quickly passing away, shall be given to the evil; but he will give the coming age to the good, because it is great and eternal."[5] It is the new age, the other age, the *eternal* age; for it does not belong to time, but is coming when the times shall have been fulfilled. "Then all times and years will be destroyed, and from that time on there will be neither month nor day, nor even hours."[6] Then all that is perishable will perish, death will be slain, and all that is subject to decay will decay. Indeed, there, where there is no longer such a thing as time, even the memory of this time will disappear.[7] One will no longer think of all that has made this age a time of misery. The new age will totally overcome the past of the old age.

The time of eternal peace will dawn, and the golden age of Paradise will return. God will dwell in the midst of the blessed. Sin, as the root of all evil, will be eradicated, so that "from this time forth forever sin shall no more be mentioned."[8] The righteous, who will find entrance into that age, "will all become angels in heaven, their faces will shine with joy."[9] They are like the stars and wear the clean garments of celestial brilliance.

Thus what is involved in the coming age is not an exalted continuation of the old age, but an entirely new, different age. The old heaven and the old earth with its creatures will pass away, and God will create a new world, a new heaven will appear, and the whole creation will be renewed. Peace will then take the place of war, light will replace darkness, and eternal joy will replace death. "In the future world there is neither eating nor drinking, neither propagation nor increase, but the godly sit with crowns on their heads and rejoice in the brightness of God."[10] The old eon knows no abiding peace, its ways are uncertain and slippery. "But the ways of the great age are broad and sure and bear the fruits of life."[11]

In many apocalyptic circles the difference between the two ages is especially emphasized in that the two world-courses are seen in the framework of a dualistic total outlook. History is accordingly determined by a cosmic struggle between God and his adversary.

In some cases the adversary is portrayed as the fallen angels, who according to Gen. 6 mingled with the children of men and begot the host of demons, the cause of sickness and the ones who lead people astray into idolatry and other sins. This conception dominates, for example, the Ethiopic Book of Enoch, which knows the angels Azazel and Semjaza as the leading figures of the evil powers.

More frequently, however, the figure of Satan, still almost unknown in the Old Testament, appears in apocalyptic literature as the adversary of God. In the apocalyptic writings he usually bears the name Beliar or

Belial, in the Old Testament an abstract concept for uselessness and wickedness. This Satan can be presented in mythical fashion as a monster, so that the final struggle of the old age is waged as a struggle against the dragon. But Satan can also assume historical contours and appear in the form of feared rulers such as Antiochus IV Epiphanes, Herod the Great, or Nero, in whom Satan appears masked, the tyrant in the end-time of the old age.

Not all apocalyptists venture to set a mythical rival in opposition to God. Any trace of the just-described dualism is lacking in 4 Esdras and in the Syriac Book of Baruch. For that dualistic outlook signifies a dangerous threat to the sovereignty of the Old Testament God and calls into question the unitary character of the course of history. Only with the help of a determinism, according to which God allows Satan as his fallen creature to hold lordship for an already predetermined period, can these dangers to some extent be avoided.

But where dualism appears, it succeeds in making visible in convincing fashion the contrast between the two ages. This evil age stands under the dominion of Belial and his demonic host; the devil is called, apocalyptically, "the god of this age" (2 Cor. 4:4). The old and the new ages are as far distant from each other as God and Satan, light and darkness, life and death. The beginning of the coming age therefore goes hand in hand with the total annihilation of the existing age, and thus of the Satanic power. "And he (God) himself will wage war against Belial" (Test. Dan. 5:10). But along with the devil, sin and sickness, suffering and death, godlessness and perishability disappear. God again dwells among men, and his good angels care for them.

We are readily inclined to stretch the difference between the two ages into the schema of this world and the beyond. But if we do that, we allow a false feature to distort the apocalyptic conceptual picture. Both ages stand under the influence of powers from "beyond." The contrast between this age and the other is the opposition of Once (or Now) and Then, of Formerly and Subsequently, of Past and Future. The apocalyptists do not think in spatial terms, but in temporal ones, though in this, to be sure, time—characterized positively as well as negatively—is also comprehended in quantitative terms; the old and new ages have their definite, already determined times, they have their boundaries and limits in time, they are allowed a *place* in time, beyond the limits of which they cannot go. But it is a matter of places in *time* which succeed one another *in* time, both of them wholly determined by this world and yet also wholly determined by the world beyond, even though "that" age is characterized by the fact that eternity, understood as timelessness or as endless time, replaces time.

Even the struggle against the devil, the ruler of the old eon, is in fact waged by *God* as a battle that in principle belongs to the "beyond." That is to say, man cannot conquer this powerful opponent of God. The succession of the ages comes about as a battle of the powers of the beyond that reaches into this world.

The pious person therefore can only *wait* for the dawning of the new age. *God* will bring it in. But he does not need to wait much longer. The reversal of the ages is imminent. "For the youth of the world is past, and the full vigor of the creation is already long ago at an end, and the advancing of the ages is almost here and even past. For the pitcher is nearly to the fountain, the ship to the harbor, the caravan to the city, and life to its close."[12] Only fools can fail to see the signs of the times; for signs of the upheaval are present in great numbers. When the old creation passes away, this does not happen without violent death throes, and the birth pangs of the new time are sorrowfully intermingled with the death struggle of the old world.

The eon that is passing away is visibly aging; "for the world has lost its youth, the times are approaching old age."[13] Hence the circumstances and conditions in the world are growing ever worse.

The people of the end-time are weaklier than their predecessors.[14] Birth deformities increase in number.[15] Children are born as old men.[16] Epidemics spread and dreadful illnesses rage.[17] Women will soon cease bearing children.[18]

The earth loses its fruitfulness; seed does not grow to harvest.[19] Poverty and famine spread, and conditions of society become intolerable.[20] Rain ceases to fall.[21] The springs dry up.[22] The birds fall silent.[23] The wild beasts come out of their hidden lairs.[24]

Sun and moon leave their regular courses.[25] The stars collide.[26] Signs proclaiming doom become visible in the heavens.[27] Blood flows from the trees, and the stones cry out.[28]

The end of the whole creation has come; God has laid the ax to its roots; its death struggle begins.[29] Anyone who has eyes that are open sees the omens of the end heaping up in the present and visibly increasing from day to day.

In addition to all the signs in nature, there is the shocking increase in human depravity. Human relationships are confused. "The wise are silent, and fools speak,"[30] for "reason goes into hiding, and wisdom flees into her chamber."[31] Therefore new wars are constantly breaking out.[32] Even brothers fight against each other; fathers and sons are in opposition to each other, and the social order collapses.[33] The terrors of the end are being announced in the present; the old age is moving toward its end with quickening step.

It can also be read from the entire course of history that the end of the old eon is now imminent. History indeed has a definite duration that has been set by God—as a rule one reckons on six or seven thousand years from the creation to the end, and thus a world-week—and on the basis of indications from the Old Testament one can speculatively calculate that the time of the old age must be nearly fulfilled.

Seeing one's own place as coming at the end of time becomes especially clear, of course, when one divides the course of the world into individual epochs. In such a division the sacred numbers, which are also widespread elsewhere, find their application: four, seven, twelve, and seventy-two (or seventy). All these are connected with the course of the year, namely, with the four seasons, the seven days of the week, the twelve signs of the zodiac, and the seventy or seventy-two five-day weeks. Daniel, for example, divides the course of the world into four parts. The golden, silver, bronze, and iron ages follow in succession (Dan. 2, 7), and the symbols chosen show how the course of the world is moving steadily downward, toward the bitter and inescapable end. The four empires appear in the picture of the four beasts, the last of which has ten horns, and then another little horn comes up among them: this is the last ruler of the fourth world empire, the Syrian king Antiochus IV, with whom, in the apocalyptist's opinion, the end now comes. According to Ethiopic Enoch 10:12, the old eon is to last for seventy generations, and the reader knows that he belongs to the last generation. Of course, this generation now must endure the catastrophe of the end and enter into the kingdom of God, the coming age, through great tribulation. The evil have more than earned the tribulation. The judgment will come upon them anyway. But the great distresses of the pious grieve God. Therefore he will shorten the times by causing time to move more quickly to its end.[34] The pious can also bring about the end by means of their constant prayers and cries; for God will not allow the cries of his elect, which come up before him day and night, to go unheard (Luke 18:7).

Therefore one should by no means be grieved over dying before the end. For thus one escapes the fearful horrors and judgments of the old creation which writhes in the death throes, and will be able to enter at once into the unblemished new age. For at the beginning of this age the dead will rise, so that the living will have no advantage over those who are dying or have already died. "The earth will give back those that rest in her, and the dust will release those who sleep therein. The chambers will restore the souls that are committed to them."[35] For "my judgment is to be compared with a ring; in it the last are not behind, and the first are not ahead."[36]

According to the Ethiopic Book of Enoch[37] the righteous will be delivered from the final distresses by a deep sleep. Then cosmic upheavals of the greatest magnitude will take place. The old world burns up in the fires of the world conflagration or drowns in the great flood.

The hellish prince of this age will not willingly surrender his power. He summons all his vassals, the demonic angel-powers and the earthly tyrants, and tries to drag the whole world down into his corruption. But God preserves his elect ones.

And when God has defeated Satan, then "the world will return to the silence of the primeval time, for seven days, as in the very beginning, so that there is no one left. But after seven days the age which now sleeps will awaken, and perishability itself will pass away."[38]

Opinions differ as to whether *all* the dead will arise. The evil, of course, would only arise to a judgment anyway, a judgment which would condemn them again to death, the second death, from which there is no return. Hence it is not unusual to find the view that only the righteous would rise again; for "the Most High has created this world for the sake of many, but the future world only for a few."[39]

Of course, the hope of the resurrection is not constitutive for apocalyptic. Occasionally we find the idea that only the last generation of those who live will participate in the new age. These living ones are called blessed because of what their eyes can behold.[40] Such a conception, which holds no hope for the deceased, can all the more easily be endured, the closer one sees the upheaval of the ages approaching, and the more surely one counts himself as belonging to the last generation. But, on the whole, apocalyptic is marked by the expectation of the resurrection of the dead, that is, by an expectation which already in Jesus' time had gone beyond actual apocalyptic piety and had become the mark of the pious orthodox Jew and a distinguishing mark, for example, between Sadducees and Pharisees.[41]

THE ESSENCE OF APOCALYPTIC

In the first chapter we attempted to sketch something like an apocalyptic "system," in the form of a survey of the most important conceptions which constitute the apocalyptist's view of the world and of history. It is true that these individual conceptions, as we shall see later, are for the most part not originally apocalyptic; hence they are also by no means unitary. But one must not overlook the fact that in their apocalyptic context they form a relatively complete whole. By virtue of their coming together to form the apocalyptic view of the world, they acquire a specific meaning, and for this reason it is now our concern to comprehend this specific meaning, which is expressed in their totality as well as in detail; that is, the "essence" of apocalyptic. In this connection one must show whether the presupposition is correct that in apocalyptic we are dealing with a unique religious phenomenon, that is, with a specific understanding of the world, of history, and of existence.

Apocalyptic was quite early recognized and labeled as an entity of a distinctive kind; this was done first of all by giving the name "apocalyptic" as a characteristic designation to specific apocalyptic *literature*. This assignment of the name appears to be of Christian origin and can be documented beginning in the second century. It presumably goes back to the beginning of the only apocalyptic writing which found acceptance in the Christian canon, the "Revelation of John," which begins with the words, "Apocalypse [= revelation] of Jesus Christ, which God gave to him to show to his servants, of what must shortly come to pass. . . ." In this assignment of the name one oriented himself on what has to qualify as "apocalyptic" literature by means of the most important *formal* characteristic mark of the corresponding writings: the revelations are imparted to their recipients by means of visions—only rarely by auditory experiences—whether in a dream, by means of ecstatic vision, or by means of rapture with an accompanying heavenly journey.

Since this formal identifying mark applies to the great bulk of apocalyptic literature, even though not exclusively to it, it is understandable that the originally literary concept "apocalyptic" was maintained for the later-emerging religiohistorical description and, by ruling out such revelational writings as give expression to a type of piety differing from the apocalyptic type, was employed to identify the *religious phenomenon* of apocalyptic as we have sketched it in the preceding chapter. In this terminological process we find expressed the conviction that apocalyptic is a relatively closed, cohesive, and independent religious phenomenon. Regardless of the source of the individual ideas and concepts which were adopted by apocalyptic, they were put to the service of the "apocalyptic" understanding of the world and man, of God and history.

The Essence of Apocalyptic

How are we to understand this apocalyptic as regards its "essence," as religion? In other words, how are we to understand the apocalyptic type of *piety*? How did the believer in apocalyptic understand himself in the midst of his world, in the presence of God, in association with other people, and in the present time between past and future?

First of all, it is striking to note in what a radical fashion the apocalyptist oriented himself to *history*. Cosmic data and processes are only of peripheral interest to him, and this exclusively in their significance for interpreting and judging the course of history. As we have already seen, this holds true for the extended astronomical chapters in the Ethiopic Book of Enoch, on the basis of which the assertion has often been made, incorrectly, that apocalyptic has an independent cosmological interest. But one should observe how, for example, at the very beginning of the Book of Enoch the cosmological statements[1] are surrounded by the portrayal of God's historical dealings.[2]

The apparent unchangeability of the cosmos which God created suggests to the recipient of the apocalyptic message that God's plan for history also, which the apocalyptist is disclosing, moves with unfailing certainty, that the judgment is coming, without any doubt. "As your Father's will is in him and as your will also is in you, so also the intention of my will for all the future stands already complete in me. . . ."[3] This plan for history holds the collective interest of apocalyptic literature; for the reality and truth of the world is shown, according to apocalyptic thinking, to the person who inquires as to the *world's history*.

A comparison with the Greek idea of the world makes

it clear how far from self-evident such an understanding of historical reality is.

When someone asked about the encompassing reality of being, the Greek referred him to the cosmos. In the cosmos everything that is real is arranged in order spatially, and in this context "order" means "in good order." Gods and men and things have their respective "place" in the cosmos, and if they do not abandon this place, but are fitted into the order of the cosmos, they themselves and the world are "in order." The word "cosmos" originally meant "ornamentation," and in fact in religious devotion the Greek admired the splendid harmony of the cosmic order which can be perceived by every "rational" man, since every man has a share in the world-reason which pervades the entire cosmos and shapes it, the "nous."

The order of the cosmos has its existence independently of the course of time and of history. Whatever may happen can only serve to restore the disrupted order and to place itself and things in their own proper place in the world. Insofar as the Greek reflects on history in its course, he teaches us to understand the past because the future will follow a course that corresponds to the past. And a glimpse of the whole of history, a rare thing for the Greek, teaches him that this whole of history runs as in a circle, so that what happens is repeated from age to age. The question as to the *meaning* of all that happens cannot be raised for one who knows, prior to all occurrences, the eternally grounded order of being of the cosmos that is at rest in itself. His goal is, out of all tragic disturbances, to achieve rest and calm, which corresponds to the unchanging order and regularity of the world; eloquent expression is given to this goal above all by the creations of the Greek artists.

The Essence of Apocalyptic

To behold the harmony of the cosmos, both great and small, signifies for the Greek the highest blessedness. In contradistinction to the current Greek view of the world, apocalyptic is in the highest degree historically minded. Everything that happens stands in a great *temporal* context. Insofar as one will speak of an ordering of reality, it is a matter of an ordering in time. It is not an order of being, but history that lies exposed to the eyes of the apocalyptist when he surveys what has been and what is to come.

But the apocalyptist is not concerned with a backward-looking or foreseeing view of history; and only when we gain this insight do we begin to understand him. In relation to the dramatic unfolding of all that happens he takes a stance of disinterest, even of remoteness. He does not marvel at how God has so wondrously governed all things. He does not reconstruct the context of history because he wants to assign every detail to its meaningful place and thus to understand history as having meaning. He does not pursue a philosophy of history, and even the question as to the meaning of history in general would presumably have thrown him into a state of confusion.

To be sure, such reflection on the whole of history is possible only where one comprehends reality as history and claims to have an overview of this history and consequently to be able to understand it in terms of a unitary whole, moving toward a goal. Therefore the Western philosophical and religious interpretation of history unquestionably grew, directly or indirectly, out of the thinking of apocalyptic. But the apocalyptist himself still did not raise the question thus. He did not set himself over against history, and did not make it his object, regardless of how surely he was persuaded that he could survey it from the perspective of its final end. He did not explore from without in search of a meaning, an inner necessity in the course of history. He did not arrive at the idea that history had to follow its past course out of a substantive necessity. The modern idea of development is foreign to him.

As the Greek sought his place in the cosmos, at the same time, of course, admiring the cosmos in its transparent beauty and harmony, so the apocalyptist inquires as to his share in the obscure, enigmatic, and painful course of history. He does not wish to know where he is to fit into the good cosmic order, but what hour has struck for him in the evil world, and he learns and makes known that his hour is the last hour of the old eon; the hour in which everything, everything, will change; the hour of radical transformation; the hour of revolution, in which nothing of the old remains and all is renewed; the hour of the final battle, the last judgment; the hour longed for and hoped for by the pious, the hour in which salvation is dawning; the hour feared by the evil, in which corruption is coming upon them; the hour of the death struggle of the old world and the birth pangs of the new.

The author of the Fourth Book of Esdras, deeply moved by the question "How long yet?", when he inquires as to the relationship of the past to the remaining time of the old eon, receives the vivid reply:

Stand to the right, and I will explain to you the meaning of a parable. And when I stood there and saw, behold! a blazing furnace passed by before me, and when the fire was past, I saw how the smoke still remained. Then a cloud full of water passed by before me, which sent down a mighty rainstorm. But when the rainstorm was past, some drops remained still in the cloud. Then he said to me, "Consider for yourself; just as the rain is more than the drops, and the fire is more than the smoke, so also the measure of the past has been greater by far; but there are still remaining—the drops and the smoke."[4]

Thus: "If you survive, you shall see it, and if you live long, you will marvel. For the eon is hastening fast to an end."[5]

The apocalyptist's thought is intensively *historical*, that is, he very strongly conceives of himself as a historical being who finds himself only when he comprehends *when* he is living. This is demonstrated, not so much by the interest in history in general, which could in fact be a detached, curious, speculative interest, as it often appears in modern times, but by the apocalyptist's concern about the hour which is striking for his generation. And when he discovers that he is undoubtedly living in the time of great transformations, which will leave nothing unchanged, his historical understanding of reality also becomes recognizable from this; for in fact he sees himself and his circumstances as subject to change in a radical way, and to the highest degree.

Now, of course, on the other hand one can point out that the course of history is in fact determined by God. Is the historicality of man still taken radically if man's decisions are without influence on the course of history? One can in particular give special emphasis to the point that according to apocalyptic, the turning point of the eons is God's concern alone, entirely independent of the decisions made by man.

Is the historicality of man preserved if he himself

cannot bring about a change in his own fate? Before it is suggested, in view of such considerations, that apocalyptic clearly forfeits the claim to historicality, two things ought to be considered.

In the first place, one should observe that the apocalyptist does not arrive at his view of history as predetermined from some nonhistorical or arbitrarily chosen historical point of view, but at a particular time, namely, at the end of history. Thus the idea of predetermination does not serve to get a grasp on the nature of history in general and to say to man how things stand for him at any given time; if that were the case, history would be understood after the analogy of the Greek cosmos, and man could do nothing but adjust passively and impassively to his fate of the moment, as his history might confront him.

For the apocalyptist, however, the idea of predetermined history as a whole is a guarantee of the *special* character of *his* present. In the face of the regular, unchanging, eternally fixed, and divinely directed course of the world, he can have the irrefutable certainty that he stands at the end of time, will soon have history behind him, and will experience the great transformation. Thus it is precisely the predetermination of the course of history that makes it possible for *him* to have a historical attitude: his thinking and hoping, his activity and his way of life, are determined by the exceptional situation of the historical upheaval in which he is living. Even if for the rest he would and could, with a superabundance of his own power, bring about the turn of the ages, *now* this is no longer possible for him, because the time of the old eon is fulfilled anyway. He lives in a time that is without comparison or parallel.

Thus the potential threat of the loss of history, which undoubtedly issues from the determinism of apocalyptic, is to a great extent rendered inactive by the apocalyptic expectation of the imminent end. Of course, this threat was bound to have its effect accordingly when the end failed to appear and the pious apocalyptist had to reconcile himself to a continued course of history after the expiration of all the dates that had been set. Thus relatively early[6] we encounter the principle "All the dates have come and gone; now it is only a matter of repentance," a view which diverges from that of the strict predetermination of the end and therefore was already being disputed among the rabbis toward the end of the first century,[7] but obviously possesses the significance to make possible a historical attitude beyond the expectation of the end. A precisely corresponding function is served by the rabbinical assertion that Israel needs only to keep two Sabbaths and it will be redeemed without delay.

To be sure, assertions like those cited are found only on the periphery of apocalyptic, in the rabbinical literature. As a general rule, indeed, the later apocalyptists no longer indicate a point in time at which the end will come, and they warn and exhort the believers to be patient and watchful, but they do not reckon that it is in man's power to bring about the end. Every present time remains a potential end-time. The end is never pushed off into the distant future, and so the historical tension is maintained.

The already mentioned catchword "repentance" leads us to the second set of problems to be considered here. Certainly the end now is coming without human contribution. Man will *experience* the new eon, but will not bring it in. Yet the really crucial question, whether the individual will have a share in the new world, is left to his decision. At the end of the Syriac Apocalypse of Baruch we read:

> For lo! when the Most High shall bring to pass all
>   these things,
> There shall not be there again a place of repen-
>   tance, nor a limit to the times,
> Nor a duration for the hours,
> Nor a change of ways,
> Nor place for prayer
> Nor sending of petitions,
> Nor receiving of knowledge,
> Nor giving of love,
> Nor place of repentance for the soul,
> Nor supplication for offences,
> Nor intercession of the fathers,
> Nor prayer of the prophets,
> Nor help of the righteous.
> There there is the sentence of corruption,
> The way of fire,
> And the path which bringeth to Gehenna.
> On this account there is one Law by One,
> One age and an end for all who are in it.
> Then He will preserve those whom He can for-
>   give,
> And at the same time destroy those who are
>   polluted with sins.*

Here we see clearly with what immense historical responsibility man is burdened in this present last time;

*85:12-15. English translation from *Apocrypha and Pseudepigrapha of the Old Testament*, ed. R. H. Charles, Vol. 2 (Oxford: The Clarendon Press, 1913). (Hereafter cited as Charles.)

everything is now being decided, and it is up to each individual to determine how the decision turns out. It is true that this historical "Now" could not be brought about by man, but it is up to him now to choose definitively between life and death: what a historical choice! Still the radical dehistoricizing of the future, in which it appears that there will be no more historical decisions, serves to heighten the radical historicizing of the present moment, and hence it may by no means be claimed to cause a general loss of historical character for apocalyptic.

The recipients of the Book of Baruch belong to a community which has already decided against *this* eon and for the exclusive expectation of the now approaching *heavenly* age: "Now when you receive this epistle, read it in your gatherings with care and meditate on it . . ."—with these words Baruch begins the closing section of his book. But the readers must *stay* with this decision. They may not abandon the community which is awaiting the eschatological salvation, may not be reconciled again to this present age, and must also win those who are undecided and in doubt by using the words of this book. Their times demand a constant and supremely important historical commitment.

Hence, in a way entirely uncharacteristic of the Old Testament, the length of life can be declared irrelevant, because the decision between life and death is a matter of the *moment:*

> With the Most High, length of days does not count for much, nor the fact that one's years are few. For what profit was it for Adam that he lived 930 years, since he still transgressed the commandment that had been given to him? Thus the long time that he lived profited him

nothing; instead, he brought death and shortened the years of those who are descended from him. Or what loss was it to Moses that he lived only 120 years, since because he was submissive to him who created him, he brought the law to the descendants of Jacob and lighted a lamp for the race of Israel.[8]

In brief: if by historicality we mean man's power ever to achieve in the present historical decisions in which he himself is at stake in the midst of history, then we cannot speak of a loss of history on the part of apocalyptic. To this extent, then, the fact that the predetermined past and the decisionless future appear unhistorical does not argue for a nonhistorical consciousness on the part of the apocalyptist, since he does in fact live historically precisely in that he relates all history to his present lot and understands this his present in a unique way as the time of decision, that is, in an eminently historical sense.

Of course, all this does not mean that those scholars who speak of a more or less significant loss of history on the part of apocalyptic are utterly incorrect. Such a dehistoricizing is undoubtedly found in the apocalyptic picture of the world insofar as the apocalyptist is unable to appropriate any intelligent responsibility for the present age, the tangible world, current history. This world is corrupt from its very foundations upward, so that everything that develops in it deserves to disintegrate. There is no hope at all for the bettering of this age, and if God alone had not set an end for it, one would have to put up with whatever his time brings. One can only wait for the end of this age and hope that it will come *soon*. Thus the apocalyptic way of looking at the world and at history is thoroughly pessimistic.

This pessimism finds its expression, among other places, in the assertion, foreign to the Old Testament, that sin and, as its consequence, death, came into the world through Adam and drew all men inescapably into their fate.[9]

Thus, for apocalyptic, creation and history are separated. God did not create history, but Paradise. Therefore God's intention in creation was definitively canceled by Adam's fall. Out of Adam's sin grew history with its trouble and woe, from which only the new creation can liberate mankind.

This pessimism, which doubts any significant worth for the course of history which is moving to its end, sets the necessary context for understanding the apocalyptist's urgent inquiry about when the end will come, his *necessary* longing to experience the end soon, and his inescapable conviction that the end is imminent.

Inextricably bound up with this pessimism and prompted by it is also the conviction that the coming age is utterly unlike the present one that is passing away, so that there is no continuity between the Now and the Then, and only after the total collapse of the present eon will the new one be produced by God, as a new creation out of nothing. Out of this antagonistic setting in opposition of the old and the new, the now and the then, arises the fact, already noted, that the new age is described precisely as *nonhistorical* and that for the apocalyptist it is the greatest comfort to know that in the new age the righteous will even forget the old one and will consequently live "without a past." We have already said that this nonhistoricality, which is only to be expected and which becomes especially evident in the loss of one's own past, by no means dehistoricizes the apocalyptist's own present time, generally speaking; instead, it rather serves to set in bold relief the decisive character of the imminent end-time. But, at the same time, this characteristic view of the nonhistorical nature of the coming age, insofar as it is regarded as an essential feature of apocalyptic dualism, is connected with that loss of history which we have considered and which is unmistakably revealed in the radical pessimism toward history and in the abandonment of this history, even within history itself—even though it is at the end of history.

Not least, this pessimism toward the still ongoing course of history is also expressed in the mythological placing in opposition of Satan and God as the lords of the present and future eons. In addition, the lively belief in angels and demons separates God from this world-epoch. The view that the devil and his hordes rule the present course of the world corresponds to the already mentioned myth of Adam's fall and, like that myth, gives expression to the view that humanity, as a *massa perditionis*, is incapable of lifting the impending fate of death from the once good creation; even the few righteous ones cannot hope for anything for this world from their own doing, particularly since they themselves are in fact involved in the fate of sin, as their death indicates. In the last analysis man stands powerless in the face of the suffering and misery of the world, and in the conviction that the new world is to be brought in only by God the existential experience is asserted that man cannot achieve salvation, but can only await it, and hence that salvation is not to be realized of and in this age at all. But at the same time this means the renunciation of any historical responsibility for the fate of this world's course.[10]

The Essence of Apocalyptic

Here we may venture the conjecture that, in this pessimism with regard to reality that is or can be experienced, we come to the very heart or the original experience of apocalyptic thought, and that apocalyptic represents an attempt to deal positively with this experience of reality, in a definite and unmistakable fashion. This conjecture is supported when one observes that, and how, apocalyptic literature itself engages in debate with other attempts to cope with the radically pessimistic basic experience of existence.

In 4 Esdras the seer asserts:

> It would be better if the earth had never brought forth Adam, or if it at least had kept him from sin. For what good is it to all of us that we now must live in tribulation and after death have punishment yet to await? O Adam, what you have done! When you sinned, your fall did not affect you alone, but us, your descendants, also! For what good is it to us that eternity is promised to us, if we have done works of death? that an imperishable hope is promised to us, if we have so sadly succumbed to vanity? that places full of healing and peace are prepared for us, if we go thither in wretchedness?[11]

These words are filled with resignation. They refer back to the story of the fall in Genesis and interpret it in the way already mentioned, foreign to the story itself and to the rest of the Old Testament. While in the Old Testament story of Adam's fall the nature of human sin is set forth in terms of *example*, the view that the fate of sin arose through Adam's guilt serves a radically pessimistic outlook on life. "O Adam! What you have done to all those who are descended from you!"[12] It would have been better never to have been born.

Now in the just-cited assertions from 4 Esdras this pessimism leads to resignation; it ends in a nihilistic understanding of existence. In this hopeless form it does not represent the opinion of apocalyptic, but a form, apparently widespread in the environment of apocalyptic, of the pessimistic view of the world *against* which the apocalyptists set themselves. For assertions like those cited, uttered by the seer to God or to the angel who is his companion during his vision, are immediately corrected: "Adam is solely and exclusively the occasion for himself; but we all, each one for himself, have become Adam."[13] But by no means are all men sinners worthy of condemnation after the image of Adam. For example, in this sense Esdras does not belong to the "seed of Adam," and he is forbidden to put himself on a par with the sinners.[14] It is true that the host of those "who are born for nothing"[15] is as much greater in number than the redeemed as the flood is more than one drop,[16] but to these few certainly belongs the life which was offered to all. The solemn assertion is made:

I swear to you sinners: As no mountain became or becomes a slave, and as no hill becomes a slave-girl to a woman, so also sin was not sent upon the earth, but men created it of themselves, and those who commit it bring on themselves great condemnation. Barrenness is not *imposed* on a woman; it is because of the works of her hands that she dies childless.[17]

In other words, it is true that there is no hope for sinners and for this sinful age. Sin hangs on this world-course as a fate since Adam sinned, and it swells from generation to generation, until it reaches that climactic point at which the judgment inevitably devours the creation which has been consuming itself. To this extent the idea of original sin serves the apocalyptic understanding of existence. But one can escape this fate of sin: the righteous shall live. For the righteous, the boundless pessimism with respect to this age is combined with a great hope for the coming age. The absolute "No" of apocalyptic to this world-age, which can also find adequate expression in the doctrine of inherited death and whose experience of reality is, to be sure, nihilistic, still does not lead the apocalyptist into absolute resignation, but rather to a great hope for a new creation.

The loss of history on the part of the apocalyptists is shown also in the absence of any political program or proclamation related to the society. The apocalyptic circles evidently did not participate in the Hasmoneans' struggles for political freedom. In Dan. 11:34 the successful war of the Maccabeans against the Syrians is slightingly called "a small help" for the pious, hardly worthy of mention in comparison with the turn of the ages that is expected from God, and the Ethiopic Book of Enoch[18] describes the fate of the apocalyptists who are mistreated by their own revolutionary countrymen:

> They were slain and destroyed and had no hope that they would see life another day. They had hoped to be the head, and they became the tail. . . . They sought to escape them, in order to gain security and to attain rest, but they found no place whither they might flee and where they could save themselves from them.

The continuing text shows that the revolutionaries who were dominant in the country formed a solid front with those who persecuted the pious.

This repressive conduct on the part of the ruling party is understandable. A group which in principle rejected the national battle for freedom had to be regarded as an alien company in the land. But it is a part of the confession of the apocalyptists not to be able to expect anything wholesome and helpful from and in this present age, and thus even less from a war for national dignity and independence.

The apocalyptic groups therefore obviously led an existence as conventicles and, separated from the public religion, cultivated a sect-mentality, even though they occasionally gained influence in the synagogues.[19] It is not by chance that here and there in apocalyptic writings we even encounter anticorporeal tendencies, which otherwise are foreign to Judaism, and which point to the "pietistic" character of the apocalyptic movement.

The apocalyptic loss of history becomes still more radically evident when one observes that in apocalyptic literature there is a total lack of concrete, specific paraenesis. It is true that the Law remains in force—for any and every Jew this is self-evident. The pious observe the Law, and the unrighteous reject it. But nowhere is the content of the Law more precisely defined. Evidently the apocalyptic concept of the Law allowed all the diverse views of the content of the Law which flourished in Judaism, and in addition in the context of apocalyptic universalism it apparently allowed for the divine law written on the hearts of the heathen. Every Jew had some concrete conception of "law."

For apocalyptic the Law also fits into a series with other realities which the pious person heeds and the impious person rejects. Assertions like the following occur stereotypically:

For they [the sinners] have, of their own free choice, scorned the Most High and rejected his law and abandoned his ways; moreover, they have trodden under foot his righteous ones, and they have said in their hearts, "There is no God."[20]

From all this some have concluded[21] that, in apocalyptic, "law" has lost the sense of a concrete manner of conduct and has become the sign of the election of the Old Testament people of God. "Righteousness according to the law" would accordingly mean remaining in the elect state. But this national-Israelite interpretation overlooks the universalistic and individualistic turn which occurred more or less intensively in apocalyptic as compared with the Old Testament. But that opinion may very well be correct in this respect, namely, that apocalyptic had no interest at all in any specific ethical definition of the contents of the Law and did not participate in the intra-Jewish discussions about the concrete expressions of the Law, *for the reason* that in view of the end of this age those discussions were without significance. Hence, in apocalyptic, "law" is not a symbol of Israel's election but, whatever contents it may hold, is rather an expression of the will of God, before which the pious person has bowed, in order now at the end of time to receive his reward, and which the sinner holds in contempt, for which he now will be punished. The time for intensive discussion of what the Law requires in detail at any given time is now past; that person is obedient to the Law who now joins himself to the community of the believers in apocalyptic.

The Law is concretely fulfilled only with the divine plan for history. "Law" is in fact the apocalyptic faith, the turning away from history in general and the unconditional turning toward the goal of apocalyptic hope. Anyone who, trusting in the new age, in the midst of this dark world and incomprehensible fate, is in harmony with God, belongs to the company of the righteous.[22] To the apocalyptist, who searches for and explores God's plan for the world, it is said:

> Thou hast left what is thine own,
> Hast devoted thyself to what is mine
> And sought after my law;
> Thou hast applied thy life to wisdom
> And hast called reason thy mother. (4 Esdras 13:54-55)

And from the fact that God's law was burned up in the temple it is deduced: "Thus no one knows the deeds which thou hast done and which thou wilt yet do."[23]

Thus the Law provides information about God's actions in history, including his eschatological action and activity in the present end of history. In this sense Law and Wisdom constantly stand side by side:[24] The Law will convict of their folly those who take a negative stance with reference to the apocalyptic message. There appears to be no more thought at all of ethical instructions. Law means revelation in the broadest sense. And insofar as Law was supposed to be understood in a "legal" sense, it still has no current relevance, but only the function of providing the basis for judging in the final judgment.[25] The apocalyptist is not moved by the question what now is to be done in concrete ethical terms. "The time is near. Let the evildoer be evil still, and let him who is filthy be filthy still" (Rev. 22:10-11). Even an interim ethic for the last fragment of the world-age is lacking. Thus in this respect too the abandonment of history on the part of apocalyptic cannot be overlooked. If one starts out from the fact that the apocalyptic understanding of existence is essentially determined by a radical pessimism with respect to the reality that can be experienced and a resignation with respect to its own inability to alter the course of the world, one must therefore speak of the loss of a significant dimension of history. Nevertheless the apocalyptist does not fall victim to pessimism in such a way that he becomes a nihilist, but he possesses a hope which is not less radical in its character than his pessimism. This combination of unconditionally negative and absolutely positive aspects is made possible by the dualistic doctrine of the two ages. The pessimism is oriented to this world and involves the possibility of man, who has succumbed to this world and therefore can only increase the measure of evil. The optimism is oriented entirely to the coming eon and hence to the possibility of God, who alone is able to check the misery of the present course of the world, but will undoubtedly do so in the near future.

In the fact that in this comprehensive historical dualism the decision between the two ages is made possible for the individual man and is demanded of him, man encounters himself as a historical being who is capable of gaining or losing his future.

In this intermingling of man's abandonment of history and his historicality there is disclosed an utterly self-willed understanding of human existence, which by comparison with other religious understandings of existence found in the environment of that time will take on discernible contours.

THE HISTORY OF THE STUDY OF APOCALYPTIC

In distinction to the literary phenomenon, the *religious* phenomenon of "Apocalyptic" as such was not discovered until modern times. Therefore the history of the study of apocalyptic is barely two hundred years old. Two barriers hindered, until the threshold of modern times, the discovery of apocalyptic "religion" as an independent sphere of investigation.

In the first place, there was lacking any historical access to the Bible and its environment which would have allowed the understanding of the individual biblical and related nonbiblical writings in terms of their unique historical place. The entire Bible was regarded as God's timeless revelation which was detached from historical differentiations: Old and New Testaments appeared on a *single* historical plane. Thus the fact remained undiscovered that there was apocalyptic as a definite religious movement between the two Testaments.

In the second place, the isolation of the biblical writings from the other literature prohibited the natural comparison of biblical apocalyptic with the nonbiblical. The sharp distinction between the inspired writings of the canon and the other, noninspired books compelled the explanation of the biblical apocalypses in connection with the rest of the biblical literature, even where an interpretation in connection with the extrabiblical apocalyptic literature would have been much more appropriate. The two more or less apocalyptic books of the Bible, the Book of Daniel and the Revelation of John, were thereby classified, not without reason, in the "prophetic" literature, which nevertheless meant the minimizing of their specifically apocalyptic characteristics.

Toward the end of the eighteenth century those barriers disappeared. People began to explain the biblical writings historically, without regard for their inspiration, and in the long run the biblical canon could not set any limits to this historical inquiry. Now all sorts of developments were discovered within the piety of the Old Testament. A distinction was made between preexilic Judaism and the so-called late Judaism of the postexilic period. It was observed that this late Judaism came increasingly under the influence of foreign religion, particularly of Parseeism.

The Book of Daniel played a large role in such discoveries. Already around the end of the eighteenth century the recognition prevailed that, contrary to its claim, this book did not come from the period of the exile, but from the second century B.C. Thus the task of determining the relationship of Daniel to earlier prophecy was posed, and in the execution of this task, at the beginning of the nineteenth century, the noncanonical apocalyptic literature came in increasing measure into the field of vision of the scholars.

The study of the Apocalypse of John ran parallel to the study of Daniel. It had already been doubted in antiquity that the disciple John had composed this book. In the middle of the third century, Bishop Dionysius of Alexandria, who disliked many of the views in the Johannine apocalypse, denied the apostolic authorship of the last book of the Bible, using Alexandrian scholarship and pointing out the peculiar language and the unique style of the work. At the end of the eighteenth century this denial was taken up again. In the vigorous discussion of the question of authorship, of course, the total character of the book was involved, and the question of the relationship of the already thus-labeled "Apocalypse" of John to the rest of the apostolic literature drew increasing attention, after the father of historical-critical biblical scholarship, Johann Salomo Semler, in his study of the Apocalypse of John had adduced the other apocalypses from the New Testament period which were known to him.

Hence it was not by chance that the first attempt at a general presentation of apocalyptic arose in connection with the exposition of the Apocalypse of John. Friedrich Lücke, a pupil of Schleiermacher, proposed to consider "the Apocalypse in pragmatic connection with the totality of apocalyptic literature." To this end he published in 1832 the *Versuch einer vollständigen Einleitung in die Offenbarung Johannis und in die gesammte apocalyptische Litteratur* [Attempt at a complete introduction to the Revelation of John and the whole body of apocalyptic literature]. We can credit Friedrich Lücke with having established the independent investigation of apocalyptic. At the same time, through his work the religious complex which was being increasingly understood as a distinctive independent area definitively acquired the label "apocalyptic," which was derived from the Apocalypse of John.

As far as the history of the study of apocalyptic is concerned, the substantive evaluation of apocalyptic made by Friedrich Lücke is of little significance. It moved along conservative lines. He held the traditional classification of the apocalyptic writings among the prophetic books to be appropriate. It is true that in his opinion in apocalyptic we are dealing with a late form of prophecy, characterized by a much greater flow of images, symbols, and allegories, and of extended ecstasies and visions. In both cases eschatological predictions, in the case of apocalyptic predominantly Christological, form the content. Regardless of how these are to be judged in detail, the abiding truth of apocalyptic lies in its universal salvation-historical perspective, and this indeed holds true preeminently of the canonical apocalyptic literature, in which the prophetic spirit speaks of Christ or through Christ, which is not true of the noncanonical apocalyptic.

This very separation into canonical and noncanonical apocalyptic shows that Friedrich Lücke did not go beyond the beginning point in comprehending apocalyptic as an independent religious phenomenon.

A milestone in the history of the study of apocalyptic was set by the first monograph on the subject, a study published in 1857 by Adolf Hilgenfeld on *Die jüdische Apokalyptik in ihrer geschichtlichen Entwicklung* [Jewish apocalyptic in its historical development]. Hilgenfeld, a pupil of Ferdinand Christian Baur, was a major representative of the so-called "Tübingen school" which had been founded by this significant theologian. The chief merit of the Tübingen school was that of carrying through the idea of development, primarily in its presentation of the history of primitive Christianity, but also beyond this in the whole history of Christian dogma; dogmas too have their history, which according to the Tübingen view advances chiefly in the Hegelian three-stage cycle of thesis, antithesis, and synthesis.

Hilgenfeld now remarked that if one wishes to portray in terms of developmental history the emergence of Christianity out of the Jewish soil where it has its roots, the canonical combination of Old and New Testaments distorts the historical problem; "between Old Testament prophecy and Christianity there is at least no direct connection."[1] Between the Old Testament and the New there lies, as the actual native soil of Christianity, late Judaism, which according to Hilgenfeld's opinion was predominantly marked with the apocalyptic stamp. Thus, in terms of the developmental history, in the investigation of primitive Christianity apocalyptic occupies an extremely significant position. "Only in the Jewish apocalypses do we have reliable documentation for the status of the Jewish expectation which Christianity found at hand. Jewish apocalyptic is the historical mediation between the religion of the Old Testament and Christianity, because between the Messianic *hope* of later Judaism and the Messianic *faith* of Christianity there was, from the very outset, the very closest contact."[2] Hilgenfeld therefore places his study "in the perspective of a *prehistory of Christianity*," and for this reason he gives his book the subtitle "Ein Beitrag zur Vorgeschichte des Christenthums" [A contribution to the prehistory of Christianity]. In his opinion "Jewish apocalyptic actually represents the entire prehistory of Christianity." "Nothing else takes us so far into the actual birthplace of Christianity as does the pattern of thought of Jewish apocalyptic."[3]

The historical judgments as to the role which apocalyptic played in the emergence of Christianity naturally imply a substantive judgment as to the essential nature of apocalyptic and of the primitive Christianity which was closely related to that apocalyptic. Hilgenfeld attempts to identify and define this nature of apocalyptic, "the inner unity . . . , which includes and embodies in itself all the peculiarities of . . . apocalyptic,"[4] by applying himself exclusively to *Jewish* apocalyptic, since the further shaping of apocalyptic piety in the Christian sphere represents a topic of the history of Christian dogma, not of the prehistory of Christianity. "The only way, however, in which this unity of essence which is expressed in a multiplicity of phenomena can be found is *the historical emergence* of this apocalyptic"[5]—a methodological principle which impressively demonstrates the intensively *historical* thinking of the "Tübingen school."

For Hilgenfeld, as for Friedrich Lücke, apocalyptic grows out of Old Testament prophecy. In it we are dealing with an *"imitation* of prophecy," prompted by the longing of the age that had no prophets. Since "the fresh surge of the religious spirit which created for itself the prophetic form and freely shaped it"[6] was no longer available, there resulted, by an inner necessity, the compulsion for pseudepigraphic composition. And because apocalyptic arose in the middle of the Hellenistic era, in which Israel was involved in the destiny of world history, the national aspect was unavoidably bound to be displaced by the universal-historical aspect. A sensible development of the apocalyptic thought-world leads from the Book of Daniel by way of the Jewish Sibyl from the second century B.C. and the Book of Enoch (around 100 B.C.) down to the Fourth Book of Esdras, which was written about the beginning of the Christian era. The development reached in the Ethiopic Book of Enoch and in 4 Esdras, "to the pure and sharp opposition of a poisoned, self-dissolving Here-and-Now and a future, a Beyond, which will appear after the total collapse of this world,"[7] brings us thus to the beginnings of Christianity. "The gospel had to be preceded by that yearning for a total reversal of things, for a decisive purification of conditions in Judaism, a yearning which is expressed in the last two apocalyptic writings; and the expectation of the future had to be elevated above the popular Jewish version to that level of a wholly new, imperishable creation, so that the gospel with its call, 'Repent, for the kingdom of heaven is at hand,' could gain acceptance."[8]

The merits of Hilgenfeld's study are manifold. He treats apocalyptic strictly historically; in the process, the boundary set by the canon finally disappears. He—like others before and after him—judges apocalyptic to be an imitation of ancient prophecy, a view with which we must later concern ourselves in some detail. He consistently holds apocalyptic to be the mother of Christian theology, thus proposing a clear solution for an important and still disputed problem; we shall also have to return to this issue for separate consideration.

Further, he strove to discover the historical development within apocalyptic itself. Now, it may justifiably be doubted whether he has carried through with this undertaking successfully enough. For one thing, Hilgenfeld hardly places Ethiopic Enoch and 4 Esdras correctly as regards time; moreover, our sources, which are only very scanty, do not suffice for us to be able to write a convincing history of apocalyptic. But Hilgenfeld's achievement reminds us to take into consideration the fact that to a certain degree the concept "apocalyptic" represents a modern scholarly abstraction. Scholarship must continually redefine what the term covers and to what extent we must make historical distinctions within the phenomenon which the term succeeds in identifying in broad terms.

The chief drawback in Hilgenfeld's presentation lies in his *one-sidedness* in fixing it historically. Because he ties it to Old Testament prophecy in one direction and to primitive Christianity in the other, he is interested in apocalyptic primarily as an intermediate link in a developmental history, and correspondingly less as a religious phenomenon in its own right. Thus apocalyptic is not evaluated as contingent actuality in history, but only as a moment of historical development, which is irrevocably superseded by this development itself. But does the picture of steady historical advance into new possibilities, in which the past is taken up into new actuality, a picture which underlies such historical thinking, correspond to the actual history? Does not repetition also belong to history? Are not historical realities at the same time historical possibilities, potentialities? Does not the apocalyptic view of the world and of human existence to this extent remain historically present? These questions do not come to the attention of Hilgenfeld, for whom apocalyptic flowed into the course of history and thus was taken up historically—but not preserved for future historical possibilities.

Around the beginning of this century the study of apocalyptic was wholly dominated by the "Religionsgeschichtliche Schule" (history-of-religions school). This theological tendency was interested in understanding the Christian religion as a special instance of religion in general, whereby Christianity in general served as the highest stage of development of religious reality. In this sense, with the religious historians the historical interest was combined with the phenomenological investigation of religious problems. Thus, while the representatives of the history-of-religions school were interested simply in the phenomenon "religion" and in this sense also in the history of religion, still they knew very well that religion as such can be viewed only in concrete historical religions. In that connection, because of its position between the two Testaments apocalyptic forms a favorite territory for the work in the history of religions primarily pursued by Protestant theologians and philologists.

In the first place, the history-of-religions school is interested in the history of apocalyptic religion itself, to be sure not so much in its inner development as in its connection with religious currents outside Judaism. In that connection, the already long-observed ties with Iranian religion are reviewed with particular intensity; but Babylonia, Egypt, and Hellenism also enter the students' range of vision. Thus apocalyptic is regarded as a phenomenon of the general history of religions.

So we see that the ancient problem of the historical and substantive connections of apocalyptic with the Old Testament and with Christianity is repeatedly taken up anew and, seen as a whole, provided with a unitary solution. The point of departure ordinarily is the question of the relationship of prophecy and apocalyptic. As was already the case with Adolf Hilgenfeld, the apocalyptists are regarded throughout as the unfruitful epigones of the prophets. In comparison with the prophetic heroes, the apocalyptists appear as "puny dwarves. There, flourishing life; here, drab theory; and only seldom does one detect the warm pulsebeat of their life; for the rest, they nourish themselves on the past." Thus writes Hugo Gressmann in a book (1905) on the origin of Israelite-Jewish eschatology.[9] People speak of the apocalyptic fantasies of rare saints, of bizarre, grotesque forms in which late Jewish syncretism is expressed, of apocalyptic late Judaism as a religion of decay and dissolution. And the more critical these judgments are, the more clearly do Jesus and early Christianity emerge from the fog of that strange, decaying, and degenerate religion into the light. "Before the unity and vitality of authentic and true piety could once again emerge from the seething chaos, one had to come who was greater than apocalyptists and rabbinical theologians, and a new formation had to emerge in the form of the gospel," writes Wilhelm Bousset, the patriarch of religiohistorical research.[10]

Finally, then, the religiohistorical school is interested in apocalyptic religion as such. Following Schleiermacher, the historians of religion had recognized "religion" as an independent life-force, and their labors ultimately tended to represent the Christian religion—properly understood—as the summit and consummation of previous religious development. It was no longer merely the historical significance but the independent religious value or disvalue of apocalyptic piety that drew the attention of the student of religion. The religiohistorical school's standard work on late Judaism, written by

Wilhelm Bousset, characteristically bears the title *Die*
Religion *des Judentums im späthellenistischen Zeitalter*
[The *Religion* of Judaism in the late Hellenistic Period].

Indeed, as we have already seen, the value of
apocalyptic religion was little esteemed. With the de-
rogatory historical estimate of apocalyptic between
prophecy and primitive Christianity, at the same time a
critical judgment was passed on apocalyptic as religion.
What the apocalyptists communicated "was for the most
part not their own material; it was tradition which they
had received and poorly reworked, made up of material
pulled together, often without plan, from here and there,
an interweaving of often irreconcilable ideas. With few
exceptions (Daniel, 4 Esdras, for example) it lacked any
personal stamp. Thus in spite of all the self-assurance of
their hopes, ultimately they only helped to make
apocalyptic a labyrinth in which the Jewish hope wan-
dered from generation to generation."[11] To be sure,
"there is something gripping and touching about seeing
these devout apocalyptists at work."[12] In the midst of an
increasingly legalistic Judaism they "preserved for
Jewish religion a bit of inwardness, a quality of honest
yearning and powerful longing for God." But even this
"something" remained veiled, lying in the hands of
epigones and clothed in fantasy, until it "came into the
hands of the Master."[13]

Such a judgment will hardly do real justice to
apocalyptic. The significant historical impulses which issued and still issue from apocalyptic do not grow out of a
degenerate substratum of the prophetic movement. But
the imported conception of the essence of true religion
hindered the historians of religion from making a more
objectively correct estimate of apocalyptic piety. The

theologians of the history-of-religions school adhered for the most part to the liberal theology. With the concepts "religious personality" and "religion of morality" the major criteria of the liberals' understanding of religion are given. Neither of these two criteria could be verified in apocalyptic. For unlike the prophets and unlike Jesus, the apocalyptists were not tangibly evident as religious personalities. The historians of religion incorrectly evaluated the fact of the pseudonymity of their writings as the authors' insight into their own status as mere epigones: "Of course, they did not have the courage of conviction of the ancient prophets; without exception they wrote under borrowed names of ancient men of God."[14] And even though the fantastic apocalyptic hope of redemption did cling to the idea of redemption, still this idea did not take the necessary "ethical-joyous turn" which Jesus first gave to it as the founder of the "ethical religion of redemption." Thus one was bound unavoidably to arrive at a relatively negative evaluation of apocalyptic religion.

However, it remained the merit of the history-of-religions school that it taught us to understand apocalyptic as the expression of a vital religious experience, and it may be affirmed that, as a result of this beginning, the nature of apocalyptic piety is more profoundly understood in our century than previously. To be sure, the fact that the historians of religion viewed even apocalyptic through the medium of the concept of personality hindered their access to the real heart of the apocalyptic understanding of existence. Most of all, apocalyptic's understanding of history remained unnoticed, and hence its picture was one-sidedly drawn; for the dualism and the hope of the future on the part of apocalyptic are correctly understood only in connection with its evaluation of history.

The way was paved for a change in the evaluation of apocalyptic when the insight prevailed which Johannes Weiss, carrying through strictly religio*historical* thinking, had already expressed in 1892 in a study entitled *Jesus' Preaching of the Kingdom of God*. This insight was that, contrary to the assumption of the liberal historians of religion, Jesus by no means preached that the kingdom of God had dawned in ethical personalities, but that he expected the imminent inbreaking of this rule of God in the Jewish-apocalyptic sense. In this way not only was the Jesus of the nineteenth century given back to his own time, but a more positive estimate of the apocalyptic native soil of primitive Christianity was also suggested.

In various works Albert Schweitzer worked out the sketch of a "thoroughgoing eschatology" of primitive Christianity. Jesus announced the now-approaching kingdom of God of apocalyptic anticipation. Out of the delay in the fulfillment of such expectation arose Christian theology, which in its Pauline form explains that the kingdom of God is already invisibly at hand, present in the power of the Spirit, and is developing toward its visible manifestation. Therewith, Schweitzer explains, the supernatural kingdom begins to develop into the ethical kingdom, and to be changed from something to be expected into something to be actualized. We have to follow this course to its end and to bring about the coming of the kingdom by seeing to it that the Spirit of Jesus comes to power in our hearts and, through us, prevails in the world.

In this sketch of thoroughgoing eschatology, it is true,

Schweitzer turns the apocalyptic view back again entirely into the liberals' ethical interpretation of the kingdom of God, but he does this in a positive relation to the original apocalyptic historical thinking of Jesus and of primitive Christianity.

Even Rudolf Otto, who discovered the Holy-Numinous, the Irrational of the idea of the divine as a specifically religious category, one that is fundamental for all religions, moved from this evaluation to an increasingly positive estimate of "the great spiritual content of late Jewish apocalyptic."[15] It appeared to him that in apocalyptic "the operative factor was an idea necessary to religion, and necessarily pressing its way more definitely into consciousness, viz. the idea of the transcendence of the divine over all that is of this world. It is the idea of the wholly other, the supramundane, which was first worked out in a mythical form in the contrasts between, and in the spatial superposition of, two spheres, that of earth and that of heaven."[16] Thus apocalyptic stands for the basic religious idea, "that righteousness, as a state of sanctification, and that blessedness are not possible in an earthly form of existence but only in the wholly other form of existence which God will give; that they are not possible in this age but only in a new age; that they are not possible in the world but only in heaven, and in a kingdom of heaven."[17]

But it is not only the dualism of apocalyptic that is positively interpreted in this essentially appropriate way. The eschatological orientation of apocalyptic piety too is gratefully and in some places even passionately seized upon. "Jesus preached: The time is fulfilled. The end is at hand. The kingdom has come near. It is quite near. So near that one is tempted to translate: It is present. At least, one can already trace the atmospheric pressure of that which is ready to break in with mysterious dynamis. From its futurity it already extends its operation into the present. It is perceptibly near." Thus writes Rudolf Otto[18] also, and proceeding from similar exegetical observations Karl Barth at the same time formulates it thus: "If Christianity be not altogether thoroughgoing eschatology, there remains in it no relationship whatever with Christ."[19]

It is undoubtedly true that apocalyptic and its eschatological orientation are very differently understood in the thoroughgoing eschatology of Albert Schweitzer, in the general religiophenomenological orientation of Rudolf Otto, and in the dialectical theology of Karl Barth. Common to all of them, however, is the attempt to find a positive point of contact with apocalyptic, whose distinctiveness all the theologians mentioned derive, with good reason, essentially from the apocalyptic understanding of history.

With these remarks, however, we find ourselves already in the present time, in which is to be observed a lively interest, fed from various roots, in investigating the apocalyptic understanding of history. In the apocalyptic situation of the Second World War, H. H. Rowley wrote his book *The Relevance of Apocalyptic* in England. He saw the enduring significance of apocalyptic thinking above all in the warning not to confuse the possibilities of man with the possibilities of the kingdom of God: "Our schemes of reconstruction are couched almost wholly in economic terms, and we make the capital mistake of supposing that an economic paradise would be the millennium. . . . Yet the apocalyptists did not for a moment imagine that the kingdom of God would be established by human means. It could be established only by a divine act."[20]

Nowadays, precisely opposite to this, under the direct or indirect influence of Marxist thought, often mediated through Ernst Bloch, the demand is not infrequently raised to bring into history the apocalyptic utopias of the new creation and as far as possible to realize them with the help of changed economic conditions. The "principle of hope" raised by the apocalyptists as a standard is to be understood as the principle of action and is to guide in the realization historically of the kingdom of liberty. A "theology of hope" conceived by Jürgen Moltmann attempts to domesticate even in theology this historical thinking inspired by apocalyptic.

With greater theological deliberation, but not without genuine passion, Ernst Käsemann reminds us that apocalyptic was the mother of Christian theology, which a church can deny only to her own detriment. Christianity is saved, by her apocalyptic roots, from dispensing "solutions for today without taking into account the possibilities of the imminent morrow or of the distant future. . . . That exodus from established positions which characterizes the Church in its true being has never taken place without apocalyptic hope and warning."[21] Käsemann does not intend this reference to apocalyptic to be understood in Moltmann's way as justification of a theological system entirely shaped in terms of apocalyptic. Instead, he is referring pragmatically to the apocalyptic soil in which Christianity is rooted, in order to warn the "pilgrim people of God" against becoming satisfied with what has been achieved and hedging itself about with conservative tenacity.

The theological program of "revelation as history,"

primarily connected with the name of Wolfhart Pannenberg, is constructed in a significantly different way; this program does refer back repeatedly and emphatically to the apocalyptic conception of history, and it has called for and stimulated the study of apocalyptic to a noticeable degree. The representatives of this theological tendency are oriented to the universal outline of history given by apocalyptic. Just as the apocalyptist knows history as a whole because the part not yet enacted was revealed to him by God, so also the representatives of the conception "revelation as history" can survey the totality of history, for they understand the fate of Jesus as an anticipation of the end of all history, and the resurrection of Jesus as a prolepsis of the end-events.

It cannot be our task here to make a more detailed presentation and, when occasion might arise, to criticize the above-mentioned and related theological proposals of our day, all of which are oriented to the apocalyptic understanding of history. The fact that they sharply diverge from each other points to an understanding of the apocalyptic concept of history that is by no means unitary. Common to them all, however, is the attempt, convincing in principle, to open up the essence of apocalyptic from the perspective of the apocalyptic understanding of history, an undertaking to which in fact our own presentation also is consciously committed.

Along with the already mentioned systematic outlines, one frequently encounters today the historical question, which has been active since the beginnings of historical study of apocalyptic and is not yet definitively settled, as to the origins of apocalyptic thinking. This question is always connected with the interest in the apocalyptic concept of history; people want to render understandable the apocalyptic understanding of history by examining its historical roots. The studies of Otto Plöger, Gerhard von Rad, and Peter von Osten-Sacken, mentioned in the Bibliography, are predominantly oriented to such an inquiry.

APOCALYPTIC AND THE OLD TESTAMENT

In apocalyptic we are dealing with a Jewish movement which can be documented starting from the second century B.C. Therefore the Old Testament writings necessarily belong among the historical prerequisites of apocalyptic. Moreover, the authors of the apocalyptic writings *consciously* place themselves in the Jewish tradition. The authorities in whose names they issued their revelations are without exception figures out of Judaism's past: Enoch, Ezra, Daniel, Jeremiah, Baruch, and so on. The picture of world history which underlies their abstracts of history comes from the Old Testament and the Jewish legends which are built on it. In harmony with the individualistic and universalistic tendency of apocalyptic, the "righteous elect" are not, it is true, the members of the Old Testament people of the covenant generally; in spite of that, however, they are in fact identified with the—pious, in the sense of apocalyptic—Jews.

To be sure, at first glance the lack of Old Testament

quotations in the apocalyptic literature is puzzling. Naturally the language of the apocalyptic writings is thoroughly permeated with echoes of the Old Testament. But generally speaking the Old Testament as such is not cited. When in Daniel 9:2 reference is made explicitly to Jer. 25:11 ff. or 29:10, and the seventy years of the Babylonian captivity, mentioned there, are interpreted by the Book of Daniel to mean the seventy week-years of the apocalyptic time-reckoning, we are dealing with an exception to the rule.

Does the extensive abstention from Old Testament quotations indicate a demonstrative detachment from the Old Testament? Not at all! It is rather that the fictive historical position of the respective author as a rule does not allow an *explicit* reference to the Old Testament. "Enoch" and "Moses" can hardly quote the prophets, even if they allegedly foresaw what would happen. (On the other hand, when Daniel in exile quotes Jeremiah, who had prophesied in the preceding generation, this is quite acceptable!) Besides, what we have in the apocalyptic texts is always the repetition of instructions which the apocalyptist is supposed to have received from the mouth of God or his angels. God and his heavenly messengers, however, can hardly appeal to the Old Testament in order to give their utterances the necessary authority. Thus we may by no means infer a critical attitude toward the Old Testament tradition from the abstention from citations of the Old Testament.

On the other hand, one may not conclude from the apocalyptists' intention to place themselves within the Old Testament tradition that they actually agree with this tradition, nor even that they possibly were not conscious of modifying the faith of their fathers in definite fashion. The theologians from whose work the individual writings and strands of tradition in the Old Testament resulted intended to *interpret* the traditions already available to them. Even the prophets did not intend to say anything fundamentally new, but to render contemporary the traditional faith of Israel for their respective times, by listening to God's voice. Thus in their sayings they constantly refer to the religious traditions of Israel, to divine blessings and legal ordinances. This fact makes it permissible, with all due recognition of the diversity of theological perspectives in the Old Testament, still to speak of *the* Old Testament faith and to this extent to compare apocalyptic with *the* Old Testament, as we propose to do.

Now, in contrast to the authors of the Old Testament, and in contrast even to the prophets, the apocalyptist emphasizes that he has a new, previously unknown revelation to bring forward, one that had not been considered in the Old Testament witnesses. According to the Syriac Book of Baruch Jeremiah receives from God the command to go to Babylon with the exiles. Baruch, on the other hand, receives the instruction "But you remain here on the ruins of Zion, and I shall make known to you what will happen at the end of time."[1] Thus the apocalyptists know more through Baruch than Jeremiah was able to proclaim. They are the messengers for the last, the crucial, time.

Thus for apocalyptic the whole truth only now comes to light, since the hidden books have become manifest, books which proclaim a *new* truth, and are not merely proclaiming the old truth for the present time. It may very well be that the consciousness of the newness of his message is connected with the fact, undoubtedly not accidental, that the apocalyptist generally proclaims his views as coming from the mouths of those pious figures of the Old Testament who have no literary remains to show. Apparently he knows that the new literary form in which he speaks is demanded by the newness of the matter which he is bringing forward. Thus no comparison of the apocalyptic statements with specific Old Testament utterances is suggested to the reader; for as a general rule the apocalyptists' authorities did not speak in the Old Testament. The apocalyptic writings in fact replace the Old Testament as the final revelation.

In this connection one should also consider the fact that religious truth as ultimate, comprehensive interpretation of reality is understandably always represented as ancient, eternally valid truth. The claim that it is simply saying something new is, as a rule, by no means a recommendation for a religion. It may be asserted all the more surely that the apocalyptist felt and experienced his knowledge as new even in comparison with his Old Testament–Jewish tradition; for his stress upon the verification of his message by the acknowledged Old Testament is only secondary in nature, and he appeals first of all to the legacy of pious Israelites which is indeed ancient, but previously unknown and transmitted outside the canon.

And if *he* was not aware that his proclamation was not adequately covered by the traditional authority of the Divine Word, still it was obviously the Jewish theologians who set the boundaries for the canon of the Old Testament, whenever and however this was done. Only one apocalyptic writing, the Book of Daniel, gained admission into the Old Testament, and indeed this was not because of, but in spite of, the apocalyptic passages in this book, because people placed the prophetic author in the time of Jeremiah and Ezekiel and rightly understood extensive passages of the book in which preapocalyptic traditions were incorporated as expressions of orthodox Jewish piety. Indeed, the Book of Daniel primarily portrays the exemplary pious man who through obedient observance of the patriarchal laws secured the visible blessing of God even in a heathen environment. It is characteristic that "Daniel" nevertheless could not be kept among the scriptural prophets and was fitted into the last part of the Hebrew canon, among the "Writings."

Even among the books which appear in the Septuagint beyond the Hebrew canon no explicitly apocalyptic works are found, and the Septuagint even regularly places the Book of Daniel in the last place among all the writings. Thus, to a large extent, official Jewish theology dissociates itself from the apocalyptic literature, as also the preservation of the apocalyptic literature of late Judaism is to be credited above all to certain Christian circles who used this literature, in part in revised form. The rabbis quote no apocalyptic literature at all, apart from the canonical Book of Daniel! From all this it follows that already very early a difference between Old Testament and apocalyptic thought and faith was observed. Whether this was a correct observation, and to what extent it was correct, is our question. This question also includes the problem whether or to what extent one can set the Old Testament as a unity in opposition to apocalyptic.

If one wishes to answer this question, it will not be of much help to determine how much of the apocalyptic concepts and ideas comes from the Old Testament, how much from other religious currents, and how much from original imagination. Old Testament motifs can be used to express belief that is utterly alien to the Old Testament, while alien expressions and images in changed times can be sensible or even necessary expressions of Old Testament thought. This is not meant to dispute the fact that apocalyptic's world of concepts and language, which in comparison with the entire Old Testament is to a great degree novel and extraordinary, might also signalize a novel understanding of existence. But one will do well, if one wishes to determine apocalyptic's nearness to or distance from the Old Testament, to inquire as directly as possible into this understanding of existence, and to distrust any statistics of the occurrence of concepts and ideas.

When this is done, the fact emerges first of all that like apocalyptic, the Old Testament views reality essentially historically. The pious man of the Old Testament, when he asked about the meaning of the world, did not admire the order of the cosmos, but looked at the course of history. Creation culminates in the forming of man, that is, in the setting in motion of history. Man is not to be fitted into the cosmos as a part of it, but is to make it historically serviceable to himself. Where is there, in the time of the Old Testament and even beyond, a way of writing history that is comparable to that of the Old Testament, and particularly one that took as its subject, not individual historical events, but the course of history from the very beginning onward, in a succession of new sketches? What takes place in the wanderings of the patriarchs is not primarily a series of changes in location, but historical migrations; local references such as

"Egypt" and "land of Israel" denote in the Old Testament diverse historical qualities; the yearly festivals of Israel are historically anchored. Israel does not speak of mythical events of some prehistory which have determined in advance all that would happen, but of saving deeds through which God demonstrates, in the midst of history, his freedom to act. The prophets correspondingly expect for their respective times the decisive continuation of the history that is determined by God.

Apocalyptic, which is also entirely historically oriented, is therefore undoubtedly rooted in Old Testament piety, which also understandably places at its disposal the most material for the outlines of history.

Connected with this is the concept of God, which in the Old Testament as in apocalyptic can rightly be understood only in connection with the understanding of history. The Old Testament does not know God, as is the case in Greek thought, as part of Being, not even as Supreme Being or as Absolute Being. Since in the Old Testament reality is not at all understood in the form of an order of being in which gods and men occupy their harmonious places, but as historical existence, God too can be grasped only as being historically active. A certainly inadequate catchword like "God, the Lord of history," points to this fact. It is true that one cannot label everything that happens in history as God's direct action, but God does act historically, and he is encountered in history. All the sketches of history in the Old Testament are meant to show God at work. The best-known and, at the same time, highly characteristic definition of God in the Old Testament reads: "I am the Lord your God, who brought you out of Egypt, out of the house of bondage" (RSV).

Anyone who asks about God is referred to God's activity in history. His might is recognized essentially in that he who made history possible when at the beginning he created heaven and earth and set the stars in their courses, chooses for himself a people, forgives sins, enthrones and casts down kings, establishes and uproots nations, and that he makes wars to cease throughout the world, breaks bows, shatters spears, and burns chariots in the fire. Unquestionably the apocalyptic conception that God as the unlimited Lord of history determines in advance the course of history and the end of the old eon is directly connected with the Old Testament concept of God, which to be sure presupposes the freedom, contingency, and unpredictable character of the divine activity.

But in both places we also encounter a picture of man which is marked by historical thought. When we say with respect to the Old Testament that man is a historical being, this does not mean primarily that he, or Israel, lives at a particular place and at a particular time in history, nor that he makes history—although all this is true and is a part of his and the nation of Israel's history. It means above all that in his life he himself is at stake, that he can gain or lose himself, that he stands in decisions, in which he decides about himself. He does not bring with him into every situation a timeless, eternal being, with the concern to correspond to it as far as possible and not to disturb the harmony of all that is. He is rather his own possibility; his being is a possibility of being. He is not given to himself; instead, he is set as a task for himself to undertake. What he becomes depends on what he encounters historically and on how he conducts himself in such encounters.

It is true that in the Old Testament, as distinct from apocalyptic, the fate of the individual remains to a certain degree bound up with that of the nation, so that the historical choice of the individual does not directly determine his destiny, but it is primarily the historical conduct of the national community that determines the fate of the nation. However, this changes nothing in the view of man common to and characteristic of apocalyptic and Old Testament piety, as existing historically in the fact that he, even as a member of the nation, has his being constantly *before* him, so that any given present time is characterized as a point of historical decision.

The historical orientation to existence which is common to the Old Testament and apocalyptic is shown, finally, in the orientation to the future which is found in both. For the present we leave open the question whether or to what extent one can speak, with reference to the Old Testament, of an "eschatology," that is, of the expectation of a definitive goal of history. This question is given varying answers nowadays. But it is beyond question that the expectation of the future as such is a constitutive part of the belief in Yahweh. Since this belief confesses God as the one who is active in history, it believes in the *coming* God. Whenever God *comes,* he brings salvation or judgment to his people, and whatever is expected by way of salvation and judgment the Old Testament expects from the God who is coming. The declaration that God has dealt with his people in the past and the expectation that he will deal beneficently with them are not contradictory, but are complementary confessions of the God who is encountered historically and who *will be* what he already *has been*. Every earlier divine action carries in itself the promise of future activity. God's electing activity opens up the future, and his promising activity governs the present. The eschatology of apocalyptic, though undoubtedly radicalized in comparison with the Old Testament, cannot be understood apart from its Old Testament roots, the less so since neither the Old Testament nor apocalyptic knows anything of the cyclical view of history, dominant in the ancient world, which, following the analogy of the cycle of the seasons in nature, speaks of the eternal recurrence of the same. Instead, both understand history as linear.

However, if the world, man, and God are viewed from the perspective of history, as described, in both the Old Testament and apocalyptic, apocalyptic must be regarded after all as a religious movement that is defined by Old Testament thought and grew out of Old Testament piety.

But it is precisely this extensive common ground in historical thinking that also allows the distinctions, embraced by this commonality, in the understanding of existence held by the two forms of Jewish religious existence to come clearly into view.

We have proposed that the essential characteristic of the apocalyptic understanding of existence is to be recognized in the fact that the apocalyptist approaches this eon and his own capability of changing it with radical pessimism. He no longer holds any hope for this eon, but places all his hope in a new eon beyond history. The Old Testament knows no such pessimism toward the visible world. Perhaps the prophet Amos saw no more hope for Israel, but the lament which he voices over Israel (5:2) still does not become a lament over history itself and over the historical possibilities of God, that is, over creation as such. If Israel is rejected, it still remains a people in history like the Cushites, and cannot God also choose Philistines and Aramaeans (Amos 9:7)? Besides, Amos' predictions of disaster were not incorporated into the Old Testament without being supplemented by historically efficacious promises of blessing. The only thing comparable in the Old Testament is the pessimism of Ecclesiastes, but this book arose at a time in which apocalyptic thought also appeared, and like the latter it is distinct from the Old Testament as a whole.

The attempt has been made to regard the apocalyptic understanding of existence as a legitimate *extension* of Old Testament thinking. It is undoubtedly true that we find in the Old Testament a tendency toward an increasingly pronounced eschatology. The expectation of the future which is adapted to the belief in Yahweh is articulated ever more clearly as time goes on in the hope of a definitive saving action on God's part which will be consummated in Israel's history. To this extent the Old Testament as a whole tends toward the ultimate establishment of the kingly rule of God. In place of God's intervention in history, which is constantly anticipated in the earlier theological programs of the Old Testament, that is, in place of its constant futurity, there comes his exceptional, once-for-all action in the future. Is not the picture of the apocalyptic hope directly in line with this development that appears within the Old Testament?

This is the opinion, for example, of H. D. Preuss in his book *Jahweglaube und Zukunftserwartung:*

Even this dualistic-apocalyptic expectation is stamped, in its basic structure, by the belief in Yahweh and its expectation for the future, as indeed even apocalyptic cannot be regarded only as a case of degeneration or corruption. Instead, it is . . . by nature and legitimately connected with the eschatology and the understanding of history of the prophets in particular.[2]

Now it is true that apocalyptic is "clearly under the influence and within the legacy of the entire Old Testament and particularly of the prophetic movement," when it "is stirred by the questions as to Yahweh's plan of history and seeks to comprehend history in its unity and finality." It will not suffice, however, to affirm that apocalyptic bears witness "in a new environment and even with the help of new declaratory material to the Yahweh who prevails and who is bound up with history."[3] The pessimism toward the present historical eon in general and the utter hopelessness for the course of this world as such go beyond not only the declaratory *material* but also beyond the *expressions* of the Old Testament themselves, that is, beyond the Old Testament understanding of existence.

The postexilic Old Testament eschatology hopes for the perfecting of the creation; apocalyptic, on the other hand, hopes for a new world beyond this created world. It may be that the transitions here are fluid. The dualistic contrast of old and new eons does not appear everywhere in apocalyptic literature with the same sharpness and clarity. Hence we must return to this problem when we inquire into the origin of apocalyptic. It could be that the roots of apocalyptic lie in the immediate postexilic eschatology, so that one would have to place the crucial break between the historical eschatology of the Old Testament and the apocalyptic expectation of the end of history in the Old Testament itself. This would not affect the fundamental difference between the apocalyptic and the genuinely Old Testament understanding of history.

The Old Testament anticipates a historical salvation and therefore it can never anywhere regard man's involvement in history as meaningless, even though in the last analysis salvation is not expected to come from man's activity, but from God's intervention. In fact, it is precisely the historical saving activity expected from God that places man in a radical sense in his historical responsibility. In apocalyptic this responsibility is no longer spoken of, and indeed it can no longer be spoken of.

The apocalyptist assumes no responsibility for history. There is nothing good about this eon, and therefore there is nothing good that can be done for it. What is good lies altogether beyond all reality that is presently established.

Corresponding to this is the fact that, in sharp contrast to the Old Testament, one can no longer speak of any saving and judging activity of God *in* history. The historical books of the Old Testament tell of the great deeds in history of Yahweh, who chose his people by leading them with a strong hand out of Egypt, by giving them the Law at Sinai, by driving out the people of Canaan from before them, by establishing his king on Mount Zion, by making Cyrus his anointed one, and so on. The prophetic proclamation too was rooted in the narrative traditions, which it made timely for its own day. God has established his salvation historically, so that the account of God's history with Israel sets his salvation in motion in the present.

Correspondingly, God's judgment too is pronounced

historically; for sin and righteousness are historical possibilities.

Now, contrast this with the accounts of the history of God's people as we met them throughout apocalyptic literature—they are really devoid of theology! This view of history lacks all confessional character; it no longer knows anything of those acts of God on which salvation was based and in the light of which previous accounts of the nation's history had been constructed.[4]

Israel's salvation history becomes a chronological scaffolding which is intended to define the apocalyptist's present historical position at the end of history, so that, for example, in the Book of Daniel world history in general can take the place of the history of Israel.

Thus, in apocalyptic, history is made thoroughly secular, profane. *What* happened in history has no significance theologically. There is no salvation in this eon; how then is God supposed to perform saving acts in it? The judgment that is within history also loses its meaning. In its place appears the judgment that is beyond history: the entire old eon will burst into flame like a firebrand and pass away, in order to make way for a new creation.

The apocalyptic pessimism toward history expels God from history, to such an extent that God no longer intervenes in the course of history that is once established, and, not at all different from man in this regard, is only waiting in idleness until the appointed times are fulfilled. The devil becomes the lord of this eon. When a modern student of apocalyptic writes: "The apocalyptists believed in God, and believed that He had some purpose for the world He had made, and that His power was equal to its achievement,"[5] such a judgment incorrectly portrays the apocalyptic experience of history from the ground up. God simply has no more plans at all for this world! Therefore he does not intervene in it even with individual acts of judgment in order to move men and nations to remorse and repentance. This eon as a whole stands under the judgment of God, as will be openly demonstrated in the final judgment, when this world shall pass away.

It is only through God's withdrawal from history that history can become subject to determinism, which to this extent represents an entirely secondary motif of the apocalyptic understanding of history. The apocalyptist's primary experience consists in the dreadful view that in this eon there is no salvation and will be none. On the basis of this experience of existence, he must, in sharp contrast to the Old Testament, push God, from whom he expects salvation to come, to the periphery of history. God's activity in history, which he set in motion with the creation, is no more and no less than the range of man's capacity to act effectively in history. He does not intervene in sovereign fashion in the course of history, he makes no contingent historical decisions, and therefore he does not repent of what he has done. History is not the place of his constant mighty acts; instead, history comes to an end when he comes. God has written off history, and corresponding to this is man's disinterest in historical change. Thereby, however, history is surrendered into the hands of deterministic chronological speculation. In place of historical *activity* there appears the apocalyptist's *knowledge* about the course of history; that means, in fact, knowledge of his own historical position. The apocalyptist leaves history behind him as a smoothly functioning but at the same time functionless mechanism. In this connection some have spoken, not without reason, of a gnosticizing view of history: the dynamic force of genuine historicality disappears, giving way to a view of history which understands it as analogous to the static calculability of cosmic forces. History is interpreted by analogy with the Greek concept of the cosmos.

Apocalyptic's loss of the sense of history is most clearly expressed in its loss of a sense of salvation. For the pious person of the Old Testament, the historical anchoring of God's saving activity made every moment potentially a time of salvation. Jeremiah's comforting admonition applied even to those who were carried away to Babylon: "Build houses and dwell in them; plant gardens and enjoy their fruits," and "When you seek me with your whole heart, then I will cause you to find me" (Jer. 29:5 ff.). The pious person of the Old Testament knew himself to be sheltered in the presence of his God even in the gloomy present and thus to be blessed in the present time.

For this reason many students of the subject have regarded the late Old Testament eschatology, which anticipates a definitive saving activity of God in the future and thus pushes the present necessarily into the shadow of relative remoteness from God, as a corruption by epigones of the preexilic prophecy, which was conscious of the unconditional presence of God's grace and judgment. This view certainly is not unfounded. Thus a sharp break, tending toward apocalyptic, may already be visible in the Old Testament.

Nevertheless apocalyptic itself makes clear the difference even between the late–Old Testament eschatology and its own view of the future which overcomes history.

It does this where it integrates into its own picture of the future the Old Testament's postexilic expectation of salvation in the form of a final *historical* kingdom, in order then to have this blessed final kingdom of history be *followed* by the definitive catastrophe of the old world and the beginning of the new eon. We know this illuminating conception best from the Book of Revelation (20:1 ff.).

Since in this New Testament book the historical interregnum of the Messiah, which is followed by the collapse of this eon, lasts a thousand years, the conception described here bears the name "chiliasm." According to 4 Esdras 7:28 ff. the earthly kingdom of the Messiah lasts only four hundred years, of course; then the Messiah dies, and now the dead awake and the judgment begins.[6] Wherever the messianic time of salvation appears thus before the end of the old eon, one can very handily observe in apocalyptic the qualitative distinction between the historical expectation of salvation, as represented in postexilic eschatology, and apocalyptic's own hope for the end of history.

In harmony with this is the fact that the postexilic prophets of salvation by no means regarded their own present time as totally devoid of any salvation. Not so the apocalyptists. For them in the present there is only a *hope* of salvation; for the present, as the presence of the old eon, is simply hopeless. In the course of this world there is nothing to make life worth living; there is nothing worthy of love to be found in it. For this reason also man has no reason to offer praise, unless to praise God's determination to let this eon soon pass away. The apocalyptist *hopes* for life, love, and praise, but it is only God's overcoming of history that will bring him the hoped-for salvation. God himself has abandoned history, and this "No" of God to the present course of the world makes history the place in which only sin and death, only trouble and grief, are to be encountered—an understanding of history which is utterly alien to the Old Testament.

The fact that the antagonistic dualism which serves the apocalyptist for expression of such radical rejection of this eon is lacking in the Old Testament may be noted only in passing. It is true that in isolated places in the later writings of the Old Testament the devil appears as God's adversary, but he by no means functions there, as in apocalyptic, as lord of this eon or as a serious rival of God. Therefore the Old Testament does not deny the possibility that evil may be converted to good, while, for apocalyptic thought, good and evil are opposed just as are the two eons, without any serious anticipation of a historical conversion of evil or of the evil powers and men. Anyone who stands on the side of the godless today is in fact regarded as irredeemable:

> The good preach . . . righteousness to the good;
> The righteous man rejoices with the righteous,
> And they congratulate each other.
> But the sinners stand with the sinners
> And the apostates founder with the apostates.[7]

In these last days of the old world-age there is a historical decision possible only for the pious, namely, the decision not to go over to the side of evil and thus to forfeit the imminent salvation:

> To certain men of a generation the ways of violence and
> death are revealed; then they keep their distance from

them and do not pursue them. And now I say to you, you righteous ones: Do not walk in the way of evil nor on the paths of death. Do not approach them, lest you die.[8]

Thus in comparison with the Old Testament the historicity of man, which in principle is maintained, is in practice greatly diminished.

Finally, in this connection we must also mention universalism and the individualism which corresponds to it, through both of which apocalyptic is clearly distinguished from the Old Testament. To be sure, one should not exaggerate the difference in this respect. That God is the Lord of *all* the world is already established in the Old Testament, all the more securely the later the date, and therefore in the eschatological pictures of the later prophecies there appear also the peoples of the world, who will make their pilgrimage to Zion. And even though the individual Israelite achieves salvation only in and with his nation, still the salvation or woe of the nation depends on the individual decisions of its individual members, and especially of its leaders. Already in the Old Testament both lament and praise are prompted to a large extent by individual fate, and it is not uncommon for the prophets to assure the individual of God's judgment or grace also. On the other hand, nowhere does it appear that apocalyptic communities were formed in genuine universality outside the Jewish national community, and in apocalyptic also a modified version of the eternal election of Israel was maintained, according to which Israel is represented in fact by the pious Israelites: Israel then no longer means the legal and ethnic commonwealth but, as the "true Israel," the fellowship of the pious, the elect individuals.

Nevertheless, precisely in this fact there is displayed a fundamental shift from the Old Testament perspective. The fact that, in the fashion described, in apocalyptic thought Israel as nation recedes in comparison with the true Israel is due to the loss of the sense of history by apocalyptic, which *can* no longer do anything with the historical nation of the Old Testament; for how could the national distinctions of this eon carry over into the new creation, in which all men are "as the angels in heaven"? How could one historical entity be chosen, when in fact history in its entirety stands under God's "No"? Besides, for a long time within Israel itself the irreparable dualistic separation between the congregation of the Most High and the children of Belial had already been achieved, which left no more hope for Israel as a nation. Thus the often observed individualizing and universalizing within apocalyptic ultimately results from the dualistic-pessimistic view of history, which abandons all history together with the nation of Israel and anticipates a salvation beyond history only for individual true Israelites—which does not rule out the fact that, conversely, it was only the universalistic tendency of the Hellenistic age that made possible the apocalyptic understanding of history.

Now when we summarize the results of our comparison between the Old Testament and apocalyptic, we see confirmed what we worked out in the second chapter on the essence of apocalyptic.

Apocalyptic thinks, in principle, historically. It knows no reality that can be experienced which is not encountered as history or in the service of history. Therein it betrays with abundant clarity its Old Testament heritage. But it despairs of history itself. History is simply without hope, irredeemably lost, meaningless. Apocalyptic thought does not despair of individual situations in history; instead, there is no hope for history as a whole. Salvation cannot be realized historically at all, not even with the remnant of the pious. Only beyond history and beyond all historical possibilities does the promised land lie.

Thus is confirmed our assertion that pessimism toward the whole of historically experienced reality is the basic experience of apocalyptic and the heart of the apocalyptic understanding of existence; for in this very attitude toward history Old Testament and apocalyptic thinking differ fundamentally from each other. In the apocalyptist's conviction that he stands at the end of history there is expressed therefore the hopeful, joyous assurance that history is coming to its end—an attitude utterly impossible for the Old Testament. At the very end of history, but still standing within it, the apocalyptist expects salvation from beyond this history which is corrupt throughout, the salvation that is from God, salvation in the small circle of those pious people who have been chosen for the new eon.

The apocalyptist lives in the twilight of history and anticipates the definitive revolution which will obliterate history or will fundamentally alter the character of historical activity, in that all injustice will be eradicated and the pious will receive the kingdom of salvation.

APOCALYPTIC AND GNOSIS

When we move from the realm of apocalyptic mythology into the contemporary circle of gnostic conceptions, we feel that we have been transplanted into another world. The fundamentally historical way of thinking which binds the Old Testament and apocalyptic together is utterly lacking in gnosis. Gnosis does not think in categories of historical existence, but in categories of static being. It does not conceive the truth of reality in terms of time, but in terms of space. Human life is not characterized by the question "Where in the course of history do you live?" but by the other question, "Where are you in the cosmos of all that is?"

Gnostic thought issues from a fundamental but derivative dualism of two divine principles. Long before this world came into being, there was the opposition between a good and an evil god, between celestial light and hellish darkness. In the struggle between these two primordial powers the demonic forces succeeded in seizing a celestial light-figure. With this triumph of darkness begins the existence of the visible world. For the diabolical power intends under all circumstances to remain in control of the conquered light-figure. It therefore produces the world and mankind upon the earth. The bodies of men are to serve as a prison for the captive heavenly light. Therefore the demons break up the being from the upper world into individual sparks of light. They give to these fragments of light that consist of a pneumatic (i.e., spiritual) substance an "intoxicating drink of forgetfulness," in order to deprive them of the recollection of their heavenly home, and exile them into individual human bodies, which serve as prisons for the pneuma-souls.

Thus corresponding to the original cosmic dualism of powers of light and powers of darkness there is also an anthropological dualism of demonic body and divine soul, of mortal flesh and immortal pneuma. Since not all men bear within them a divine pneuma-spark—the demons wanted to render difficult the anticipated search of the heavenly beings for the lost part of the light—mankind is divided into two classes: the sarkics and the pneumatics, that is, those who are mere flesh, and the men of the spirit, whose real self is the spark of light that is exiled in the prison of the body.

The terrestrial world is located at the lowest position in the cosmos, farthest removed from the realm of light. Between the earth and the world of light is situated the realm of the demons, who in keeping with ancient thought are seen in the stars. These demonic powers prevent the ascent of the soul to the realm of light and guard their light-prey against attempts of the good primordial force to regain the lost portion of the light.

Naturally the light-world does not reconcile itself to the loss that it has suffered. It intends to regain the lost pneuma. Therefore it sets in motion the process of redemption. A being from the world of light makes its way downward. It clothes itself in the forms of darkness, deceives the guards that the demons have placed on the roadways through their numerous heavens, and finally reaches the earth, where it is concealed in a fleshly body or in the semblance of a body. Thus it works unrecognized among men and brings to the pneumatics among them the saving illumination about their true being, the knowledge of whence they come, how they have fallen into the power of the darkness, and how, freed from the body, they can find their way back to their heavenly home. Because he has passed through the world of darkness, the heavenly messenger in fact knows the secret of the way to heaven. After he has imparted to those who are his own the gnosis, that is, the truth about their origin and their future, he returns above along the same route by which he came down, and all pneumatics, who are in possession of gnosis, can follow him after leaving their bodies. The superiority of the light to the powers of darkness allows them even now to be sure of their redemption, to deride their demonic masters, and to hold the flesh in contempt, particularly since in ecstasy they can already anticipate the final heavenward journey.

Gnostic apostles travel into all parts of the world in order to call the pneumatics out of the sleep of their forgetfulness of who they are, and to make of them knowing ones, gnostics. When the call of gnosis has penetrated into every corner of the world, the time can be foreseen when the last light will have left the world and regained the heavenly home. Then this entire creation will have lost its meaning and it will once again collapse into the nothingness of which it actually consists, as the work of the vain and empty powers of darkness. The light-world, however, celebrates its triumph; the darkness is finally placed in check. All those who were separated are found. The end comes back to the beginning.

So much for gnosis itself. Our presentation sets forth the principal features of the gnostic mythogram, a summary of the typical ideas of the gnostic systems which in details are very widely divergent. In our subsequent statements we shall follow this ideal gnostic type and leave out of consideration in particular those branches of gnosis which are more heavily influenced by Jewish or Christian thought.

We shall not concern ourselves with the disputed question as to the origin of the gnostic mythology and religion, which must have arisen at approximately the same time as apocalyptic. We wish only to point out that categories of space and substance which are dominant in gnostic thought obviously betray the influence of the Greek understanding of reality, so that the difference between apocalyptic and gnostic ways of thinking is also immediately apparent in terms of the different roots—for the latter the Greek world, and for the former the Old Testament.

It is obvious that the categories of space and substance wholly dominate gnostic thought. The pairs of opposites which are essential for gnostic religion—truth/falsehood, life/death, salvation/misery, slavery/freedom—correspond to the spatial contrast of "above/below" or "realm of light/world of darkness," and the contrast as to substance, "spirit/flesh," "being/nothingness," "fullness/deficiency." The basic concepts of "light" and "darkness" also are used in terms of space and of substance, but not historically: the light belongs to the upper world and comes into the lower world only through a "fall"; it represents that which really is, while the darkness, by its deficiency of being, is characterized as null, void, empty. Occurrences—in the realm of gnosis one can speak of "history" only with some reservations—consist in a mixing and unmixing of substances. It is precisely this thinking in terms of space and of substance that leads a person who comes from the historical approach to thinking found in apocalyptic into a strange world.

Nevertheless, with such experience one remains in the realm of conceptions, "objectivations." In this realm there is, in fact, no bridge between a design of history which sets forth the course of events from Adam down to the present and on to the end of the world in seven or ten stages, and a portrayal of the soul's ascent through seven hostile heavenly regions or past 365 guardhouses of the demons. The gulf separating these two patterns of thought, each of which comprehensively covers the whole of human existence, is as great as that between Plato and Isaiah. But the problem is otherwise presented when one interprets the gnostic myth of the fall and ascent of the light in terms of the understanding of existence which one encounters in the myth, as we have attempted to do in the second chapter with the apocalyptic view of history. That is to say, when this is done one suddenly discovers surprising areas of common ground between gnosis and apocalyptic, which make comprehensible Rudolf Otto's judgment which originated from H. Gressmann, "Gnosis is of the very spirit of apocalyptic teaching," [1] a judgment which of course can be stated conversely as well.

First of all it should be pointed out that both gnosis and apocalyptic claim to be setting forth a *new* interpretation of the whole of reality. Since this interpretation embraces *all* reality, of course it cannot have just now emerged for the first time; what is involved here is rather the quintessential, the primordial truth concerning reality, whether of being, as in gnosis, or of history, as in apocalyptic. Therefore it is explained by both movements that the truth that is being proclaimed was there from of old, but has only come to light in the present. The apocalyptist accordingly asserts that in former times God imparted the insight into the ultimate meaning of all that happens only to a few chosen men and at the same time commanded them to publish their wisdom only at the end of time.

Gnosis, in keeping with its approach in terms of substance, starts out from the position that the pneuma-sparks, by virtue of their heavenly origin, bear within themselves the awareness of the true being. But in fact the "gnosis" is communicated to them as something new; the pneumatic must *become* a gnostic. Thus gnosis, if it wants to maintain the newness of its message, does not avoid attributing to the mass of the pneumatics a loss of memory concerning their true being. The demons are to blame for this forgetfulness of being (= forgetfulness of their true self). They have given poison to the individual sparks of light, and this has robbed them of consciousness; they have mixed for them a drink which brings oblivion; they have administered to them a sleeping potion or have prepared for them an intoxicating drink which puts them in a constant state of drunkenness. They surround them with an abundance of fleshly lusts in order to cause them to forget their origin. Hence the necessity of redemption, awakening from the sleep of death, deliverance from drunkenness, recollection of what is eternally true, guidance back to their origin, revelation of the concealed truth.

The differences between gnosis and apocalyptic are obvious. For gnosis, the knowledge of what is true is given to man along with his true *being* from the very beginning and can only be obscured by evil intrigues. For apocalyptic, the truth is disclosed only from the end of *history*, and therefore it remains unknown so long as God keeps his revelation hidden. But these differences are insignificant in comparison with the assertion, *common* to gnosis and apocalyptic, that they and only they are *now* communicating the true insight into the reality of all being or all destiny. Accordingly, both religious movements are convinced that they are bringing a new, not yet actualized interpretation of human existence. Therefore we are not surprised to find gnostic "apocalypses," so called because of their literary form, that is, gnostic revelational writings which are supposed to come from the hand of Adam, Seth, or other figures of the ancient past and which describe the gnostic knowledge as primal and primeval knowledge.

We noted earlier that, in the nature of the case, a religious proclamation as a rule does not cherish a novelty of ideas, but strives to prove the original and to that extent valid character of their truth by their age also. In view of this fact, one must ask whether the surprising coinciding of gnosis and apocalyptic in the assertion that they are not newly presenting what is true, but something new as true, is not based upon an identical experience of existence, one that is felt to be new. There is all the more reason for posing this ques-

tion since the beginnings of apocalyptic and gnosis presumably lie in the same time. What understanding of
existence is hidden behind the gnostic mythologoumenon
of the fall of the light into darkness, of the demonic origin
of the world, of man's being thrown into this existence
that is alien to him, of the assured ascent of the pneuma
into the heavenly pleroma (= fullness)?

To this question we must answer: The basic gnostic
experience consists in radical pessimism toward "historical" reality, toward this world, this eon, and to this
extent the gnostic's understanding of existence corresponds throughout to that of apocalyptic.

The first glance which is directed toward concepts,
ideas, and the historical style of thinking sees apocalyptic and Old Testament together—and together clearly
distinguished from gnosis. On the other hand, the second
look, which goes beneath the layer of objectivations to
inquire into the existential experience of reality which is
expressed in them in general and the nature of reality
which can be experienced, sees gnosis and apocalyptic as
closely related and sharply separated from the Old Testament understanding of reality.

We note first the pronounced cosmic dualism of gnosis,
which in distinction to Jewish apocalyptic does not
necessarily require the idea that the devil and his angels
were originally good creations of God who became God's
adversaries through a fall. That is to say, many gnostic
systems start out from a primordial dualism of light and
darkness, and thus deny the unity of God, which for
Jewish thought and for apocalyptic is indispensable. But
thereby it only becomes all the more clearly evident that
the terrestrial world stands over against God. The problem, difficult for apocalyptic to solve, of how this eon's

hostility to God could develop even though God alone created it and prescribed its course and its times disappears with the gnostic assumption that the world and its overseer never were on the side of light, but from their very origin and in principle are vain and empty.

To be sure, there are gnostic systems which have evil emanating from the deity. A part of the divine principle wanders away from the divine existence and activity, detaches itself from the divine roots, thereby diminishes and ultimately loses the divine being, and thus is transformed from infinite to finite, from being to nonbeing, from light to darkness, from the pneuma to the world.

The doctrine of the fall of the divine or the split in the divine world as the presupposition of the creation of the world by the nugatory powers and the imprisonment of the light-figure bears features which are akin to the apocalyptic exposition of the fall of the angels. In the Ethiopic Book of Enoch, for example, in connection with Gen. 6:1 ff. it is told that in the days of Jared two hundred angels came down to earth and mingled with the children of men, and out of this hybrid union came the giants, whose souls after the death of the giants practiced their mischief as demons.[2]

Thus with the fall of the angels evil entered into the world, the demons went into action, and the world which had been created good by God became this eon of sin and suffering. The gnostic and apocalyptic conceptions of the fall of the angels may very well go back to related mythological material, even though there are no direct connections. But this is of less interest to us than the fact that the mythological pattern serves the same purpose: it is employed to explain the negative character of the world, a character marked by hostility to God.

For this explanation it is unimportant whether the world, as in the view of gnosis, is first created by the fallen, godless powers, or whether these diabolical powers alienate from its creator the world that is made by God and place it under their own rule, as the apocalyptists explain. In the former case, the vanity and nullity of the world, in keeping with gnostic thought, is rooted in the nugatory *being* of all that is created. In the case of apocalyptic, the darkness of this eon is grounded in the *historical conduct* of the creation, which turns away from its creator. In both cases the essential quality of the world or of the course of the world is the same and is described in essentially the same words: we live in an evil world which does not belong, or at least *no longer* belongs, to God. Therefore according to both the apocalyptic and the gnostic conviction, this cosmos is destined for dissolution. For apocalyptic thought, God sets an end for it, at a previously determined time, in order to bring in the new eon. According to gnostic thought, the demonic cosmos will collapse into nothingness when all the pneuma has been released from it. It is not accidental therefore that in later versions of gnosis the end of the cosmos after departure of the pneuma can be described in apocalyptic images.

In this connection the fact deserves to be mentioned that the major role which angels and demons play in apocalyptic and in gnosis and which connects the two religious movements at the same time separates apocalyptic from the Old Testament; for in this set of facts the understanding of the world, which is similar in apocalyptic thought and in gnosis and is characteristically different from the Old Testament, becomes evident. In the Old Testament the popular belief in angels and demons is almost wholly suppressed. God is *directly* related to the world as his creation and to history as the field of his activity.

The removal of God from the world in gnostic thought or from history in apocalyptic, on the other hand, makes necessary some intermediate beings. In one case, these beings, as God's good emissaries and under his commission, mediate God's dealings with the creation which is far removed from him. In the other case, as evil beings which have fallen away from God, they form the world of gnostic mythology, a world that is hostile to God, or they govern and consummate history, which has been detached from God and whose end the apocalyptist proclaims. Thus the angelic beings, and particularly the demons, make possible the expression of the dualistic separation of God and world or of God and history by means of the then current mythology. In this way they signal the affinity of apocalyptic and gnosis in their understanding of the world and of existence; in both there appears a thoroughly pessimistic understanding of the world or of the course of this world, for which God can no longer be held directly responsible.

In anthropology, the doctrine of man, the commonality of their judgment concerning this world comes out even more clearly than in the utterances about the cosmos. According to the gnostic myth, all pneumatics—and only they are men in the true sense—are part of the light-figure which has fallen into the power of the darkness, and which therefore is often simply called "man" or "Adam." The relationship of men to the world is characterized by concepts such as "fall," "being thrown," "captivity," "alienation," "being cut off," "homesickness," and so on. Man does not originate in this world into which he has fallen, into which he was thrown against his will. He is sojourning in a foreign land, and his lamentation over the wretchedness of this world is an expression of homesickness for the world of light to which he belongs. The demonic powers have cut him off from the higher light-eon. They are keeping him in the prison of this world and in the dungeon of the body. There is no more in common between Adam–primal man or his parts and the world, between spirit and flesh, between inner and outer man, than there is between God and the devil, or between light and darkness. All the striving of the man who has been awakened out of his forgetfulness of true being and brought to himself tends toward his becoming free from this world.

The apocalyptist, who has a commitment to Jewish thought, cannot use this way of a cosmic dualism to express his judgment about the fate of man in the world. In other words, for him the world continues to be God's creation. Only in quite isolated instances do gnosticizing notes sound, lamenting not the condition of the world but the world itself, not the fallen plight of the body but the body as such; thus, for example, in 4 Esdras 7:88, where the happy prospect is presented to the pious that they may be able to separate themselves from this "mortal vessel." But it is clearly stated that God did not create man for this world of death which has fallen away from God, but for the new eon. Man sojourns in *this* eon as in exile, even though man and the world have only become alienated in the process of history. The fact that man in his sin *succumbs* to this eon nevertheless shows, just as does the gnostic's *fall* into this world, that man does not belong to this world. The same experience of existence is given expression by what is said of the fall, in terms of being and space, and what is said of the deterioration, in terms of history and time.

In that connection the mythologoumena also resemble each other in a striking way. While gnostic anthropology sees the origin of miserable humanity in the fall of Adam–primal man, the celestial light-figure who incorporates all pneumatics within himself, late Jewish literature is familiar with the "guph"-conception: Adam is the storehouse of souls, in which the number of men who were to be born was counted out as on hand from the very beginning,[3] so that the end can only come when all these men have entered into life.[4] Thus a definite time span for the old eon was set by Adam!

Corresponding to this original connecting of men with Adam is the view that all men sinned in Adam. We have already mentioned the fact that this interpretation of the figure of Adam is alien to the Old Testament itself. It is set forth in 4 Esdras in the form of a strict doctrine of inherited sin: "O Adam, what you have done! When you sinned, your fall did not affect you alone, but us, your descendants also."[5] In the Syriac Book of Baruch it is adapted to historical thought: "Every one of us has become Adam for himself."[6] Both methods of interpreting Adam's fall serve the same utterance: "When Adam transgressed my commandments, *the creation was judged*. Hence the ways in this eon have become narrow and sorrowful and wearisome, wretched and bad, full of perils and bordering on great distresses."[7] A grain of evil seed, sown in Adam's heart, has borne immeasurable fruit and has made this eon an eon full of grief and affliction.

Once again we leave open the question whether there

are reciprocal influences between the gnostic doctrine of the fall of the primal man–Adam as the sum total of all pneumatics and the late Jewish–apocalyptic implication of all men in the Genesis story of the fall. We shall content ourselves with saying that these two undoubtedly related mythological conceptions are pursuing the same intention: they explain and justify the radically pessimistic attitude of gnosis and apocalyptic toward the existing world or toward the history that can be experienced. They explain the gnostics' flight from the world and the denial of history by the pious representatives of the apocalyptic movement. This eon, along with all that belongs to it, deserves to be rejected unconditionally, whether because of its quintessential nullity as a consequence of its having been made by the demons (the gnostic view), or because of its historical wickedness as a consequence of its having been seduced by the demons (the apocalyptic view). World and history alike are viewed as totally empty of God, as hopelessly devoid of life, destined for annihilation. Everything evil comes from the world or from history. There is salvation for man only if he escapes from history and the world.

In apocalyptic as in gnosis, however, man can actually escape from history. In this respect these two religious streams share a distinction from the contemporary hopeless pessimism, for example, of Ecclesiastes and of philosophical skepticism.

Of course, in the area of this problem the differences between gnosis and apocalyptic are clearly evident. On the basis of his pneumatic being the gnostic stands apart from the world in principle. His involvement in this world is purely accidental. Light and darkness, spirit and flesh, being and nothingness cannot enter into a genuine connection with each other. In possession of gnosis the pneumatic person is able to detach himself from the world and in ecstasy to leave the body. The apocalyptist, on the other hand, by virtue of his righteous conduct takes a historical distance from this eon. He dissolves the original connection with it by means of a series of historical acts, by not putting himself on a level with *this* world, but orienting himself to the coming world. He decides not to have anything more in common with this eon, and this gives him the right, on the basis of the divine promises, to be assured that the final judgment upon the course of this world will spare him, the pious man.

Correspondingly, in gnosis the pneumatics and sarkics stand over against each other, the men "from above" and the men "from below," the former, who are everything, and the latter, who are nothing: a radical contrast which rules out all mediating positions, the difference between death and life, or between darkness and light. Apocalyptic thought knows the same contrast, though it is historically stamped, between righteous and unrighteous, between pious and godless, a contrast which is no less fundamental and definitive in apocalyptic than is the dualism of spiritual men and fleshly men in gnosis. Now, at the end of the old eon, the division among men has in fact already taken place; they have all made their decision; there is no longer a road leading from the unrighteous to the righteous. Even sympathy for the unrighteous is forbidden for the apocalyptist. King Josiah is praised because he not only killed the godless men of his day; "he also had the bones of those who had already died brought out of their graves and burned with fire,"[8] an omen of the last judgment which is now approaching, which will deliver up the world to the fire.

In keeping with its historical way of thinking, apocalyptic could not divide humanity into two classes as easily as could gnosis. But it came around to this thinking in terms of classes. For the principle "Many are created, but few saved" or "The Most High has created this world for the sake of many, but the future world only for a few"[9] is conceived and expressed to serve two purposes. It is intended on the one hand, in the context of the two-eons idea, to affirm the irrevocable division into righteous and unrighteous, and on the other hand to maintain the principle of man's historical responsibility, a principle which of course is far removed from the tendency of gnosis to think only in terms of being: man is to be held responsible for the condition of the old eon.

But these unquestionable differences between apocalyptic and gnostic anthropology are comprehended by the declaration which they have in common, that man as righteous or as pneumatic stands *over against* the world, which he holds in contempt because of its empty, nugatory nature. On the anthropological level, a class dualism corresponds to the cosmic dualism or the dualism of the eons. The class of the apocalyptic righteous men and that of the gnostic spiritual men do not share the fate of this eon that is passing away, but belong to the other, the higher, or the coming world. These classes are already in the present fundamentally set apart from the classes of the unrighteous or the sarkics.

In that connection it is individuals that the two opposing classes are composed of, and this individualizing corresponds to the universalizing of the events of disaster and salvation.

In gnosis, individualism and universalism are directly anchored in the myth: indeed, the national distinctions are found only in the realm of the "flesh," the demonic world. The pneuma is international, and the pneumatics' ecstatic speaking in tongues is universalistic. The spiritual men know and recognize each other across all barriers. The gnostics' knowledge and conduct overstride all natural boundaries. Therefore the gnosis is disseminated in all cultural circles. It conducts a world mission. The gnostics of all lands are united in the primal man.

On the other hand, Jewish apocalyptic cannot deny its historical starting point, and the election of Israel moreover belongs to this history. Jewish apocalyptic arises in Judaism and is oriented to Jewish traditions. For this reason it did not become an international movement after the fashion of the gnostic movement. It must appear all the more remarkable that apocalyptic abandons the national hope for Israel. The righteous ones are individual men, and even though in point of fact these individuals may very well have been almost exclusively Jewish, still apocalyptic was far from any limitation, in principle, of the righteous to men of Jewish origin. The forthcoming judgment will be pronounced as *world* judgment, and all men of all ages and nations will appear before the judge and will be separated into the righteous and the unrighteous.

This means that, with all the external, extensively historically conditioned distinctions, individualism and universalism are equally constitutive for apocalyptic and gnosis. Individualism and universalism are expressions of the basic experience common to apocalyptic and gnosis, that salvation lies outside this world or outside the course of this world. This is not contradicted by the fact that both gnostics and apocalyptists form a new collective consciousness: the individual pneumatics are gathered together for the restoration of the heavenly Adam–primal man; the apocalyptists understand themselves to be the true Israel, the people of the coming eon of God; for this new collective consciousness is based on the overcoming of history and of the world. The community of the pious is the eschatological community of salvation.

The understanding of existence that is common to gnosis and apocalyptic, the feeling of superiority to the vain world in the midst of this world, is expressed also in the interest in eschatology which is dominant in both movements. In this connection gnosis thinks in vertical terms, and apocalyptic in horizontal terms; but both movements think in linear terms and do not speak of a continuing cyclical recurrence of the same. To be sure, the course of the world is not understood to be uninterrupted progress. With the eschaton the circle of events is closed. The last will be like the first. Paradise will return—thus says apocalyptic; all that is separated will be reunited—thus says gnosis. But this circle will run its course only once. Fall and ascent, corruption and redemption will not be repeated. The way from the darkness to the light is not reversed. After the fall of Adam, which determined the present reality of the world, there remains only the irreversible way out of corruption to salvation.

Once again the differences are evident. For gnosis, this eon and that one are spatially separated, but contemporaneous. The way from the darkness to the light runs from here to there, from below upward. Apocalyptic, on the other hand, divides the two eons in temporal terms. It separates this eon as the present one from the coming one. The way leads from today to tomorrow, from the present into the future, from Now to Then.

But again the understanding of existence is the same: here and now man finds himself in exile; there and then he expects life and salvation. Below, as in the present, darkness rules; above, as in the future of the kingdom of God, light shines for the redeemed. Death is the state of man in the world or in time, where sin rules; life is the reward of one who leaves this world or escapes from time into eternity. It is not uncommon, in the presentation of their eschatology, for gnosis also to make use of temporal concepts, and apocalyptic of spatial concepts; but this only indicates all the more the common basic experience of existence: from this eon, from history here below, one cannot expect salvation.

Finally, the recognition of a common understanding of existence in spite of all the differences in thought and myth is confirmed when we observe how the active abandonment of history in apocalyptic which we have described in detail is repeated in gnosis. The gnostic too accepts no responsibility for this world. There is no ethical paraenesis in gnosis—a judgment which understandably leaves out of account those forms of gnosis under strong Christian or Jewish influence. The gnostic is taught to keep his distance from this world and to overcome it, whether by rigorous asceticism or by unrestrained libertinism. He is instructed in the technique of ecstasy and the ascent of the soul and is warned against the many pitfalls which the demons have set for him. But such admonitions and counsels always serve the purpose of liberation from the world, of flight from history.

Here it is easier for the gnostic than for the apocalyptist to justify this radical abandonment of history: his pneumatic being is *by its very nature* nonhistorical. Apocalyptic, on the other hand, stamped by historical thinking, requires the imminent temporal-historical expectation in order to be able to explain its abandonment of historical responsibility: the time of history is at an end. Even though a commitment to history may have been rewarding earlier, now it is no longer worthwhile.

But once again these understandable distinctions do not affect the common decision against the historical world. Like the gnostics, the apocalyptists know no ethic. An ethic presupposes a sound world which is to be preserved, or a redeemable world which is to be renewed. Ethical conduct expects salvation of or in this world. But the basic experience of existence on the part of gnosis and apocalyptic consists precisely in the conviction that there is not, and cannot be, terrestrial or historical salvation, because the world is evil to its very foundations and history is corrupt from its very beginning. Salvation simply lies beyond both world and history. Toward history, therefore, there is only the attitude of massive rejection.

Hence we must understand gnosis and apocalyptic as *radically* revolutionary or anarchistic movements. Of course, anyone who wishes to revolutionize history historically can only label the attitude of the gnostics and apocalyptists as reactionary; for the representatives of

both religions show themselves to be utterly unin-
terested in historical change. They are convinced that
one cannot give life to what is empty and vain, nor make
the evil good with the instruments of this eon, with
power and morality, with flesh and reason. In this way
they escape the tragic necessity of all ordinary revolutionaries, of being obliged to make the new world
with the instruments of the old world, and their fate of
appearing as revisionists to the revolutionary children.

Gnosis and apocalyptic engage in radical revolution.
Alteration of the world means, for them, elimination of
the world; their judgment upon this world is simply
judgment upon history; they rebel against everything
that is now dominant, and long for a world without laws;
they wholly and utterly reject what now exists, in favor
of what no eye has yet seen and no ear has heard; they
are not interested in any existing order, because nothing
is in order, and they strive for a world in which an
ordering hand is no longer required. They place God and
world in opposition and thus claim God wholly for themselves. They cannot describe the new, but they know
that everything will be different.

Thus seen, their dualism must be understood as a
dialectic of the negative. A quantitative change cannot
bring any progress to the world, regardless of however
massively it may occur. What is required is the qualitative leap into the new eon.

For this reason the apocalyptists, like the gnostics,
divide mankind into the two classes: into pneumatics and
sarkics, into righteous and godless, into revolutionaries
and reactionaries. The revolution will destroy the ruling
class of the sarkics, the godless, the reactionaries, and
will bring about the rulership of the now suppressed

righteous, the knowing ones who here are unknown and misunderstood, a rulership which will abide forever.

Gnostics as well as apocalyptists know that there is nothing good about this world. They want a wholly good world, an entirely new one. Therefore they gather the people of this new world and wait for it to come. For anyone who wants the real revolution must wait until it comes. The true revolution can only *come;* for it will liberate one *from* the world, *from* history. But it will surely come, when the time is fulfilled or when the gnostic self-consciousness has reached all spiritual men.

THE ORIGIN OF APOCALYPTIC: RELIGIOHISTORICAL CONNECTIONS

If one surveys the information that is given by the pertinent literature on the question of the emergence of apocalyptic, one has a difficult time getting one's bearings in the abundance of arguments and attempts to explain its derivation.

One can hear that in the apocalyptic literature we have to do with the esoteric literature of the learned rabbis. Other students of the matter hold the contrary opinion, that these are books of the common people which must be classified as below the level of respectable theological literature. References are frequently made to the influences from alien religions which are supposed to have determined the origin of apocalyptic; in that connection Iranian piety in particular plays a major role. Still more strongly, of course, the rooting of apocalyptic faith in the Old Testament is set forth. Some then see in apocalyptic a late form of the prophetic movement, an expression of the old prophetic piety in changed times. Others, on the other hand, emphasize the change which can be discerned between prophetic and apocalyptic theology, without intending thereby to deny a direct line of development from the preexilic prophetic movement by way of the eschatology of postexilic prophecy to apocalyptic. Can we not explain apocalyptic pessimism and the apocalyptic hope of the new eon as arising out of the disappointment over the fact that the blessed state of affairs in this world which the postexilic prophets announced for Israel has not been achieved? In that case we would have before us an immanent break in the development of prophetic thought.

Gerhard von Rad, on the other hand, places the differences between Old Testament prophecy and apocalyptic so sharply in the foreground that he must reject the derivation of the latter out of the former. He holds Old Testament "Wisdom" to be the native soil of apocalyptic and adduces weighty arguments in favor of his view.

In addition, some investigate the political and social circumstances during the period when it is presumed apocalyptic arose, in the third and second centuries B.C. This was the time when the Persian rule collapsed, Israel was drawn after Alexander's death into the political wrangling of the *diadochi*-states, and the Hellenistic spirit invaded even Palestine and captivated more than a few of the Jews. The attempt is also made to explicate the economic relationships of that time, in the expectation of being able, with the aid of sociopsychological considerations, to contribute toward solving the question of the origin of apocalyptic.

To be sure, many of these attempts at tracing the derivation of apocalyptic can be combined, whether by detecting complex causes of the clear, unequivocal system of apocalyptic, or by assessing apocalyptic itself as a complex movement with many different faces.

Intertwined in all these attempts to discover the source of apocalyptic is the question what, after all, can be achieved with such an undertaking, even if it should be successful: do these attempts explain the phenomenon "apocalyptic" by tracing its historical derivation? Can the apocalyptic understanding of existence as such be traced at all? Or, in the ways of understanding existence, are we not dealing with contingent phenomena?

If we attempt to bring some order into this mass of problems, questions, and opinions, we shall be able first of all to draw together the *religiohistorical* aspects which point to non-Jewish influences in apocalyptic. Then we shall have to consider the *developmental-historical* attempts to account for apocalyptic in essence as a development within Judaism out of Old Testament roots. Further, the *social and political* phenomena in the environment at the time when apocalyptic began must be noted and, where applicable, adduced to help clarify the question of origin.

Finally, in connection with all this, one must ask what such inquiries altogether can or cannot contribute, after all, to the understanding of the phenomenon of "apocalyptic."

The present chapter is concerned only with the religiohistorical connections between apocalyptic and non-Jewish religions, and the following chapter with the rest of the problems just cited.

It need not be questioned that many individual apocalyptic motifs of a predominantly mythological sort also appear in the religious environment of Judaism and in large part may very well have been borrowed from that source. When, for example, God's final struggle with the devil is portrayed as a battle with the dragon, apocalyptic is borrowing from age-old myths, even though we cannot determine precisely whether the decisive influence was Babylonian, Iranian, or Old Palestinian.

In the apocalyptic doctrine of the collapse of the world the ideas of a world conflagration and a worldwide flood compete with each other. It is obvious that the latter is related to the widespread sagas of the deluge. But the former also has clearly discernible roots in Eastern mythology. For example, in the Jewish-apocalyptic parts of the Sibylline Oracles we read: "And then will a mighty stream of burning fire flow down from heaven and destroy every place, the mainland and the great ocean and the blue sea, lakes and rivers, springs and the unrelenting Hades." [1]

In addition, close parallels are to be found in Iranian literature: a star falls from heaven and sets fire to the earth. The fire melts the ore in the mountains, and it pours over the earth like a stream. All men must endure this stream of fire and are purified by it; "to the pious man it is as though he were walking in warm milk, but to the godless, as though he were walking constantly in molten metal." [2]

Especially prominent in apocalyptic writings, but also known elsewhere in late Judaism, are the speculations about the heavenly places, the celestial geography, the throne of God and the attendant beings that surround him, the divine hypostases, which in peculiar fashion personify divine attributes such as, for example, Wisdom. These and similar phenomena are unknown to early Judaism and first appear—not without foreign influences—in the exilic and postexilic period. The astrological material in apocalyptic literature may very well stem in essence from Babylonian astronomy and mythology.

A similar estimate must be made of the penetration of the belief in angels and demons into postexilic Judaism. In general and in particular—for example, in the view of four or seven archangels, the belief in guardian angels, elemental spirits, etc.—alien influences are displayed along with the awakening of animistic features, among them more than a few of Iranian or Irano-Chaldean origin.

One final example: According to Daniel 2, King Nebuchadnezzar sees in a dream a giant statue composed of various materials: the head is of gold, the chest with the arms of silver, the lower part of the body of bronze, and the legs are of iron, which in the feet is mixed with clay. Daniel interprets this dream to refer to four successive world empires, all of which stand on clay feet and must now give way to the new eon. Every commentary on the Book of Daniel remarks, with reference to the four metals, the figures of the successive world-epochs, that a wholly similar presentation is found in Hesiod, in Greek thought, as well as in Iranian literature, in the Bundahisn.

But whatever we are able to show in this way of syncretistic features in apocalyptic late Judaism and perhaps even rather surely define as to their origin, for the question about the origin of apocalyptic the observation of individual conceptions and mythologoumena contributes very little. Nevertheless it is shown that the Iranian religion in particular, in the form given to it by

Zarathustra, appears to have been influential in the formation of apocalyptic, and in fact this Iranian religion exhibits a striking agreement with apocalyptic, particularly when we represent it not in individual mythological conceptions but in its total mythological outline.

Underlying this total outline is the conception of a primordial, eternal, and ineradicable contrast of two principles: the good spirit and the evil spirit, light and darkness, Ahura Mazda (Ormazd) and Angra Mainyu (Ahriman), stand opposed to each other. World history lasts for twelve thousand years and is divided into four periods of three thousand years each. In the first period the physical, empirical world does not yet exist. At the beginning of the second period it is formed as a good world by the good spirit Ahura Mazda. At the beginning of the third period the evil spirit attacks the good God and his world. Now evil is mixed into this good world. With the appearance of Zarathustra at the end of this third period the world which has fallen victim to evil begins slowly to turn again to the better. In the last three thousand years, which is the present time, the struggle is waged for the cleansing of the world from evil. This struggle will climax some day in the appearance of the world-redeemer sent by Ahura Mazda, and he will bring in the end of the world. The dead will be raised. Then all men must pass through the judgment fire which comes from heaven. The good will pass through it as through a bath of warm milk; the evil will have to suffer greatly, because the fire will purify them and burn away from them all traces of evil being. But all will finally come through the fire safely. The fire will also cleanse the earth of all evil. At the same time Ahura Mazda with his angels enters the battle against the army of Ahriman. He conquers it, and now upon the renewed earth, from which the demons are expelled, there begins a new, blessed life, free from all evil.

It is true that we arrive at this schematized picture on the basis of relatively late sources of Parseeism which cannot be dated with certainty, but it is confirmed in the essential points by the few extant remains of ancient Zoroastrian tradition and above all by Greek authors, namely Plutarch (*De Iside et Osiride*) and his authority Theopompos, who wrote in the third century B.C.

The proximity of these ideas to Jewish apocalyptic cannot be overlooked. The reality of the world is grasped in terms of world history. This history does not run in a circle of eternal repetition of the same thing, but has its beginning and end, and in such teleological historical thinking this Zoroastrian Parseeism and Jewish apocalyptic together are distinguished from the cyclical view of history of the rest of the ancient world. History spans the *entire* world, and thus is understood in a universalistic sense. The course of the world exhibits a predetermined completeness, divided up into periods. It is true that the good spirit made the world, but the driving force in history is the dualistic conflict of good and evil power. The course of the world consists in the advancing intermingling of evil with this world and its ultimate elimination from the world, so that at the end history once more arrives at the original state. Man is thrust into this struggle *as an individual*, as the judgment then also affects him as an individual. For this reason the dead must rise again.

To be sure, in the complex Iranian literature almost every one of these features is also called into question: there are remnants of cyclical thinking; tendencies toward a monistic conquest of the dualism are powerfully at work; individualism and universalism are threatened by Iranian nationalism, and so on. But such features clearly surround the system that is described, and in spite of the difficult situation with respect to the sources there can be no doubt as to the central significance of the system within Parseeism. And this central system exhibits an unmistakable closeness to Jewish apocalyptic. Precisely those apocalyptic features which cannot be derived from the Old Testament are found here: dualism; universalism and individualism; resurrection of the dead; predetermined periodically structured course of history; influence of evil in this good world; and eschatological victory of the good.

It is understandable that the representatives of the history-of-religions school, in their effort to determine the source of Jewish apocalyptic by means of religiohistorical comparisons, triumphantly point to these close connections between Parseeism and apocalyptic. Furthermore, they undoubtedly make their point when they explain the points of agreement that have been mentioned, which could be illustrated with many individual observations in addition to what has been said, with the thesis that Jewish apocalyptic is dependent upon the related conceptions from Iran. At any rate a dependence in the other direction does not come into question, for dualism, individualism, determinism, and so forth are in fact alien elements in Jewish thinking, while they constitute the Iranian pattern of historical thinking.

Is the source of apocalyptic thereby explained? One must answer this question in the affirmative if it is inquiring into the origin of most of the motifs and conceptions which are alien to the Old Testament and in which the apocalyptic understanding of existence is objectified. To a large extent the specifically apocalyptic conceptions come from Iran, and even concerning the motifs of obviously Babylonian origin it has been assumed with good reason that they first enriched the Iranian view of history and reached Jewish apocalyptic by this route.

After the Persian king Cyrus had conquered the new Babylonian empire in 539 B.C. and thereby had also subjected the Jews of Babylon and Palestine to his rule, the possibility was given for Parseeism to be combined with many Babylonian conceptions. But this was not all; above all, the Jews now came into direct contact with the Persian religion as the religion of their masters, so that nothing by way of outward circumstances stood in the way of the appropriation of Iranian conceptual material. And even the inner disposition was favorable for those Jewish circles which were open to Iranian conceptions in the formulation of the apocalyptic faith. For Parseeism was not only the religion of a politically superior power, but also that of a civil entity which was welcomed by the Jews. Cyrus permitted the Babylonian exiles to return to their home, allowed the free exercise of the Jewish cultus, and furthered the reconstruction of the temple in Jerusalem. Deutero-Isaiah had already warmly commended Cyrus as God's instrument for the liberation of his people Israel,[3] and during the time of the two-hundred-year Persian rule Judaism was consolidated as a theocratic religious community under constant favorable Persian influence. Judaism apparently at no time found occasion strongly to lament or to oppose the Persian overlordship. Iranian conceptions and ideas such as resurrection of the dead, devils, angels, and demons, divine hypostases, and so forth, permeate Jewish thinking on a broad front and not in the special area of apocalyptic alone. Hence to this extent the apocalyptists' intensive reference to Persian thought-material can easily be explained.

However, apocalyptic does not form a rare conglomerate of Jewish and Iranian conceptions, but is the expression of a specific, unitary understanding of existence. Can this understanding of existence, and thus the "essence" of apocalyptic, apocalyptic as religion, be derived from Parseeism? We must answer this question in the negative. For even though the Old Iranian dualism and the related conceptions allowed Jewish apocalyptic to give comprehensible expression to its pessimistic understanding of the world and existence, still this pessimism itself in no way stems from the Iranian religion.

The Iranian feeling for life is thoroughly optimistic. The historical world is the battleground for the struggle against the evil that has invaded. Evil is alien to the world, but man does not live in an alien, evil world. Every individual man, as long as he lives, fights the battle against evil, a battle into which Zarathustra has sent him. This battle has the certainty of total victory; for at the end, with the help of the good spirit, the demonic power will be utterly expelled from the earth upon which it has exerted its influence unjustly. Evil is unquestionably taken with utter seriouness in Iran. But the Zoroastrian religion by no means abandons this world to the Evil One, or to evil. The two-eons doctrine of Jewish apocalyptic, which modifies the Parsee dualism to the extent that it sets two world-courses in antagonistic confrontation, is not found in Iran. Eduard Meyer writes, "For the Iranian the birthday is the greatest festival, and his very existence is a vigorous affirmation of life."[4] The apocalyptist's lament over existence remains foreign to the Iranian. A sentence such as "It would have been better if we never had come into the world than now to live and to suffer in sins and not to know why"[5] stands in sharp contradiction to Zarathustra's understanding of existence. Every man has the task of participating in the struggle against evil and to further the historical influence of good by means of the increase and extension of good thoughts, words, and works.

In particularly strong optimism the Persian religion assumes that at the end all men will be saved, even though it is through the cleansing in the sea of fire—the expression of the fact that the creation and its creatures have not been corrupted by evil to the very core, but can be liberated from evil and are to be freed from it as far as possible in constant historical engagement and commitment. Evil attacks the world, but the world does not irrevocably fall victim to evil, as is the case in Jewish apocalyptic thought. Whereas for the apocalyptist the judgment brings the final separation, the definitive victory of the now oppressed righteous over the unrighteous, with Zarathustra the idea of judgment serves to prompt the constant historical decision of all men against evil. Accordingly, the Iranian also knows nothing of the apocalyptic expectation of the imminent end. This is particularly significant: thus the follower of Zarathustra does not yearn for liberation from this world that has hopelessly fallen victim to evil, but regards the course of the world in which he stands as meaningful, because in it he can successfully fight against evil. It is not the world that troubles him, but the evil in the world. He does not wish to overcome the world, but to liberate it and to win it back from evil. Therefore the teaching about the periods of history does not serve, as in Jewish apocalyptic, to identify the present age as the time of the end, but to explain the destiny of the world in general and to characterize the present as the time of the historical struggle against the evil that has invaded the world. The eschatological views give encouragement for this struggle, because they let it be seen as successful.

Hence it follows that Jewish apocalyptic in large measure fell back on the conceptual material of the dualistic Zoroastrian religion because this material allowed it to give suitable expression to its own understanding of existence, which was truly foreign to the Old Testament—a phenomenon which was repeated in gnosis, likewise influenced in considerable measure from Iran. But the apocalyptic understanding of existence itself, like the gnostic one, can by no means be derived from Parseeism, and one must not minimize this fact with the comment "The moods vary," as Wilhelm Bousset, the patriarch of the history-of-religions school, does.[6] This means a shift in focus; for what is displayed in the apocalyptic pessimism with respect to historical reality is not a slightly shifted mood within the context of an essentially constant religious attitude. Instead, there is revealed in the changed "mood" a fundamentally different understanding of the world and of existence, in spite of the widely identical conceptual material in which this understanding of existence is being objectified. Therefore the successful search of the representatives of the history-of-religions school for the source of the apocalyptic conceptions which are still foreign to the Old Testament does not actually succeed in accounting for the phenomenon of Jewish apocalyptic, and we must not conceal this fact by speaking unreflectively of Iranian "apocalyptic" only because in the religion of Zarathustra too the course of the world as a whole, including its end, is interpreted. Apocalyptic's understanding of existence is as far removed from that of Zarathustra as is the vital consciousness of a victoriously ruling people from that of a subjugated and oppressed nation.

In view of all this, should we take the opposite direction and derive apocalyptic from a movement which possesses the "apocalyptic" understanding of existence, in whatever nonapocalyptic fashion it may give expression to this "faith"? In gnosis we have become acquainted with a religious current which, with all its outward differences from apocalyptic, obviously shares with it the basic experience of human existence in this world. Can we then perhaps derive apocalyptic from gnosis?

Against any such attempt, chronological considerations and reservations will first of all be adduced. We do not possess any certain direct or indirect witnesses to the existence of a gnostic movement in the second or third century B.C., when apocalyptic arose. Nevertheless, it is not satisfactory to rely on the silence of our tradition, and even though the assumption of a well-developed gnosis at the time when apocalyptic emerged can claim very little probability, we can by no means rule out the possibility—given the incompleteness of our knowledge of the cultural and religious movements in the Syrian-Mesopotamian region after the death of Alexander (323 B.C.)—that the gnostic movement was formed even that early in the crucible of Greek and

Eastern spirit. However, it appears scarcely conceivable
that this movement with its pessimism and its hopes
stimulated Jewish circles in the development of
apocalyptic thought.

That is to say, one then would have to assume that
incipient apocalyptic could entirely detach the gnostic
understanding of existence from the gnostic myth and
transpose it into a world of language and ideas which
goes back only to Old Testament and Iranian roots. This
would be an extremely artificial and contrived proce-
dure: according to this, from the first the future
apocalyptists felt so much at home in gnosis, with its way
of thinking—mythical, being-oriented, nonhistorical—
that they understood and recognized themselves in this
thinking. But then they completely turned their backs on
the gnostic way of thinking and its stratum of objectivation, but nevertheless held fast to the gnostic understanding of existence and clothed it in a Jewish-Iranian
garment—a process for which, so far as I know, there
are no parallels in the history of religions.

This does not mean the denial of any influence of
gnostic mythology on apocalyptic. The view, asserted in
certain apocalyptic writings, that evil came into the
world through the fall of the angels appears to me to
have gnostic roots, for example, just as does the idea
that all men are embraced in Adam and sinned in him.
This latter is a historicizing of the gnostic myth of the fall
of the primal man, and the former a reflection of the
gnostic conviction that darkness developed through a
loss of light, when individual angels were detached from
the unity of the divine. Further, the figure and the name
of the apocalyptic "Son of Man," with which we shall
concern ourselves in detail later on, in my opinion pre-

supposes gnostic influence. Nevertheless, such isolated cases of syncretistic borrowing from a—presumably Jewish—gnosis do not tell us much on the question of the origin of apocalyptic, even though they are properly observed and could be multiplied. Religious motifs are quite generally subject to exchange, and at certain points nonapocalyptic branches of Judaism show themselves still more heavily influenced by gnostic mythologoumena than does apocalyptic; one may think, for example, of "Wisdom" conceived as a hypostasis, of the theology of Philo of Alexandria, of the late Jewish deification of the figure of Adam, and of the flesh-spirit dualism in the Qumran writings.

If one wishes to combine gnosis and apocalyptic in their totality in a causal relationship, a more likely case can be made for assigning to gnosis the secondary position. Such a sequence would be recommended on chronological grounds; for apocalyptic has earlier literary attestation than does gnosis. It would also be in harmony with the fact that gnosis makes use of the Old Testament in significant measure and mythologically interprets the opening chapters of Genesis in particular to support its views. There existed quite early a strong current of Jewish gnosis, that is, a gnosis which employed Jewish texts and conceptions to express a gnostic understanding of existence and undoubtedly was supported by Jews. Thus it is that in recent times an intensified effort has been made to find the origin of the gnostic movement in Judaism, especially in the world-denying apocalyptic circles. R. M. Grant, for example, has espoused the opinion that, through the fall of Jerusalem in the year 70, disappointed apocalyptic hopes had formed the decisive momentum for the emergence of gnostic thought: now, instead of being oriented to the new eon, the hope is oriented to the otherworldly realm of light.[7]

Of course, I regard these and similar derivations as wrong. The nonhistorical thinking of gnosis is so un-Jewish that I cannot conceive of gnosis as having sprung from Jewish roots, but must regard Jewish gnosis as an early and widespread branch of a movement that in its origin was pagan. But be that as it may, in any case apocalyptic cannot be derived from gnosis, even though individual mythologoumena in apocalyptic writings betray a gnostic influence. Therefore the question as to the origin of apocalyptic still remains entirely open; religiohistorical research alone, oriented to the mere comparison of motifs, is not able to answer this question.

THE ORIGIN OF THE APOCALYPTIC MOVEMENT IN JUDAISM

If the understanding of existence held by apocalyptic cannot be derived from Zoroastrian piety, even though Iran provided much for apocalyptic by way of mythological material and rational ideas, and if, for the reasons given, fully developed gnosis does not come into consideration as the native soil of apocalyptic piety, then we must turn once more to Judaism itself and ask whether we cannot understand apocalyptic in a crucial sense as a product of what was essentially a development within Judaism.

In so doing we shall not go in detail into the manifold presentations of those researchers who wish to prove an essential agreement between Jewish–Old Testament thought and apocalyptic thought—a view which we cannot share after the comparison of Old Testament and apocalyptic understandings of existence has revealed fundamental differences between the two.

Nevertheless the question remains, whether a continuous decline from the Old Testament or even within the various strata of the Old Testament toward apocalyptic cannot be demonstrated, such that the end product of this development, apocalyptic itself, was in essence detached from its Old Testament origin, without being able wholly to deny its source.

Following the precedent set by others, Gerhard von Rad has anchored apocalyptic in Old Testament piety in a specific way. Starting from the fact that the Wisdom literature also belongs to the Old Testament, and even though it also stands in close connection with the "Wisdom" of the rest of the East it is bound up with the historical belief in Yahweh, he seeks the source of apocalyptic in this Wisdom literature, which is represented in the Old Testament above all by the Book of Proverbs, Ecclesiastes, Job, some psalms, and parts of the narrative books (the Joseph stories), and then by Ecclesiasticus and other noncanonical writings.

The most important arguments with which von Rad supports his thesis may be summarized briefly:

1. The pseudonymous authors of the apocalyptic writings are regarded as "wise men" (Dan. 1:3 ff.; 2:48), as scribes (Enoch; Ezra). They deposit their knowledge in books and stress the antiquity of the learning and doctrine embodied therein. All this corresponds to what is customary in the Wisdom literature.

2. The form and content of the "Wisdom" are not specifically Israelite. Wisdom addresses the *individual* and proposes to guide him to an insight into the order and the rules governing events. The national entity "Israel" plays no role in Wisdom literature. Thus the universalism and individualism of apocalyptic are found prefigured in Wisdom.

3. While Wisdom is concerned with astronomical problems, with zoology, botany, pharmacy, and angelol-

ogy, with tides, weather, and winds, the same kind of theme appears, for example, in the Ethiopic Book of Enoch, which discloses the mysteries of nature in detail from a celestial perspective.

4. The deterministic view of history held by apocalyptic, with its assumption of fixed times and eras, corresponds to the Eastern Wisdom-thought, which ascribes to every event a fixed time and credits the wise with knowing the right times.

5. Both Wisdom and apocalyptic concern themselves with the problem of theodicy, that is, with the vindication of God with respect to the evil in the world.

On the other hand, von Rad does not attach a great deal of weight to the fact that Wisdom, as distinct from apocalyptic, does not concern itself with eschatological problems; for in his opinion "no insuperable difficulties" are occasioned by the assumption "that Wisdom, which after all does tend toward the encyclopedic, in one particular phase, probably a late one, was opened up to a concern with last things, and that in this process the assimilation of alien materials, particularly Iranian ones, also played a part."[1]

This fact reveals the weakness of the overall position of von Rad. He compares individual conceptions of apocalyptic with characteristic ideas of Wisdom and in so doing can establish, not without reason, some points of agreement; for we need not be surprised that apocalyptic as a Jewish movement also appropriated elements pertaining to Wisdom. With this method, the idea can also be formulated that at a particular time Wisdom also extended its interest to eschatological problems and to Iranian material having to do with knowledge, and was thereby transformed into apocalyptic.

Nevertheless, in apocalyptic the eschatological questions do not appear as one partial area of universal knowledge, but as a set of problems which are fundamentally determinative for the entire apocalyptic understanding of existence. The expectation of the imminent end of the world, an integral part of apocalyptic eschatology, cannot in any way be connected with "Wisdom," and it is precisely this expectation that constitutes the apocalyptic understanding of reality in general. It is true that a salvation-history [*Heilsgeschichte*] as such—that is, the history of God's salvation in this world—plays no more of a role in Wisdom than in apocalyptic; but the maxims and admonitions that are characteristic of Wisdom are crammed with a sense of history, loyalty to the community, a will to live, while none of this is to be found in apocalyptic, which instead turns away from history. The dualistic idea of eons is utterly foreign to the Wisdom literature, while it is fundamental to the apocalyptic understanding of existence. To put it briefly, if one looks not merely at the stratum of objectivation but at the essence of the piety expressive of both Wisdom and apocalyptic, one must agree with the judgment of Philipp Vielhauer: "The eschatological ideas and the expectation are doubtless primary and so fundamental that the Wisdom elements must be evaluated as colouring, and not as basic." [2]

So then the Wisdom-utterances in the Ethiopic Book of Enoch, about events in the cosmos and nature, also serve the purpose of guaranteeing the trustworthiness of the apocalyptist, who discloses the imminent and predetermined events, and therewith also the reliability of his message: Anyone who has learned so much about God so precisely surely will also be reliable about history, and if nature, which everyone can see and verify for himself, is exactly determined and calculable, then one will more readily follow the view of the apocalyptist, according to which the course of history is just as surely governed by fixed laws. Even if the apocalyptist does after all wish to make a favorable impression, by means of such proofs, on those Jewish contemporaries who are familiar with the Wisdom tradition and are committed to it, what matters to him is not the knowledge of the Wisdom itself, which is a knowledge about the order of things, but the apocalyptic insight into the course of history.

Not the least of the reasons impelling Gerhard von Rad to attempt to trace apocalyptic back to roots in the Wisdom perspective was his desire to avoid deriving the apocalyptic movement from prophetism. This negative argument forms the sturdiest support for his positive affirmations.

The very interpretation disputed by von Rad, however, that of apocalyptic as an offshoot of Old Testament prophecy, is very commonly found in the study of apocalyptic in the past hundred years. It goes back originally to the fact that the two apocalyptic books in the canon, the Book of Daniel and the Revelation of John, won their normative significance as *prophetic* writings. Thus the derivation of apocalyptic from prophecy, which one encounters in scholarly work since the end of the eighteenth century, is directly connected with the interpretation of apocalyptic literature which has been current since the canon was formed.

Besides, even von Rad does not wish to deny all connections between prophecy and apocalyptic. How do things stand with this traditional view of our problem? How are prophecy and apocalyptic related to each other? Can a decline from Old Testament prophecy to apocalyptic be affirmed? Thus, can one account for apocalyptic in terms of developmental history out of prophetic eschatology?

It appears to me that we cannot deny such a decline. We should consider first of all the fact that prophecy itself was already adding new aspects to the traditional Jewish piety. The prophets in fact declare that the Israelites in the present can no longer simply appeal to God's saving acts in the past; for they have broken the covenant which they have with God. Salvation, once offered and experienced as present salvation, retreats into the distance. The nation stands again at the "zero hour," and the prophets make it their object to make Israel conscious of this its situation, and to warn her against false security.

> The only thing she can hold on to is a new historical act on the part of Jahweh, the outlines of which the prophets already see, and to which they point with kindled emotions. The prophetic message differs from all previous Israelite theology, which was based on the past saving history, in that the prophets looked for the decisive factor in Israel's whole existence—her life or her death—in some future event.[3]

Of course, this new event is expected to be analogous to God's saving activity in the past, so far as people do not simply count on a mere restoration of the damaged saving relationships. The prophets hope for a new David, a new Jerusalem, a new covenant. However, this very hope shows that the prophets see the present as more or less gravely darkened by Israel's apostasy and seek the new deliverance in the (near) future. For this reason Gerhard von Rad is not incorrect when he speaks of an "eschatologizing" of historical thinking in the prophets, and there should be no disputing over this concept when the matter is clearly evident. It cannot be denied, however, that in this eschatologizing there is a tendency toward apocalyptic.

Then, of course, we must locate a decline even within the prophetic proclamation itself, thus structured. That is to say, in the exilic and postexilic period the promise of the imminent salvation becomes more insistent and more one-sided. In the face of the wretched situation of the nation, the preaching of judgment and the warning against false security wholly recedes. There is no present blessing of salvation which could justify such preaching. God's saving action is expected almost exclusively from the future. The present becomes strangely salvationless and remote from God. But the blessed future is at the door. Haggai and Zechariah see it as now already dawning with the beginning of the rebuilding of the temple. This coming saving action will transcend all earlier salvation, so that people can even forget the past events:

> Thus says the Lord,
>   who makes a way in the sea,
>   a path in the mighty waters,
> who brings forth chariot and horse,
>   army and warrior;
> they lie down, they cannot rise,
>   they are extinguished,
>   quenched like a wick:

"Remember not the former things,
 nor consider the things of old.
Behold, I am doing a new thing;
 now it springs forth, do you not perceive
 it?" (Isaiah 43:16-19 RSV)

In the prophets of this late period one has the impression that they anticipate a definitive saving action in which history will come to a halt. The coming judgment will sharply separate the pious and the godless, those who count on God's coming and those who deny it. The view of the eschatological pilgrimage of the nations at the same time introduces universalistic features into the eschatological picture. Thus this postexilic prophecy undoubtedly tends, discernibly and more decidedly than did the preexilic, toward apocalyptic ideas.

The approximation goes still further when the end-time—as already in Isaiah 11:6 ff., Ezekiel 34:25 ff., Isaiah 2:2-4, Joel 4:18, and then in increasing measure in the postcanonical literature—is portrayed with utopian features: as a time of eternal peace, of superabundant nature, of paradisiacal innocence, of the abolition of suffering. Therewith the end-time of history moves to that boundary of history where the change into the nonhistorical appears unavoidable. The historically possible is driven to that extreme where the impossibility of a historical consummation of salvation becomes obvious.

At the same time we observe also some formal tendencies in the later prophetic utterances which recur in the apocalyptic literature: the prophetic proclamation increasingly bears an out-and-out *literary* character, which then was entirely characteristic of apocalyptic: instead of the brief, concise messages received by hearing, we find in increasing measure the broad portrayals of visions. We may affirm with confidence that with such observations a historical decline is laid bare.

It is at this point in the historical development that Otto Plöger's fine study *Theocracy and Eschatology*, which has been accepted with a great deal of agreement, begins.[4] Plöger points out that at the beginning of the Persian period Israel changed from a people to a community, from a nation to a theocracy. Israel ceased to understand herself as a political entity, and conceived of herself as God's people, assembled around temple-cult and law. Israel became a churchlike divine foundation.

In the course of this process of transformation, the traditional eschatological expectations became superfluous. "The goal of earlier eschatological expectation, the winding-up of the nation on the lines of the plan of Yahweh proclaimed by the prophets, was in principle already attained in a community founded exclusively on cult and law; the only justification for the maintenance of eschatological hopes was that they confirmed what was, in fact, already the case."[5] Israel saw herself in the status of a salvation-community, and this status rendered unimportant the question of what future reference this present salvation possessed, in which the predictions of the prophets had been fulfilled.

But alongside these, Plöger says, there were groups who held fast to the prophetic expectation, interpreted the words of the prophets eschatologically, and hoped for the still-delayed fulfillment of the prophetic predictions. These eschatologically stirred groups inevitably came into conflict with the ruling priestly aristocracy, so that an increasingly sharp opposition developed between two tendencies in the Jewish community, each of which claimed orthodoxy for its own position.

If, then, the various attitudes to the eschatological question may be regarded as the decisive point of difference, then it is easy to see how the cleavage which is visible at this point was bound to lead either to greater indifference or to a sharper definition of the eschatological point of view. This stricter definition has obviously found expression in the conversion of the prophetic eschatology to the apocalyptic view of the future.[6]

In this process of conversion, between 400 and 200 B.C., the heirs of the later prophetic movement, who had been pushed to the fringes of the Jewish community, incorporated into their view of history in increasing measure those Iranian elements which were suited for expressing the understanding of existence which was becoming more and more apocalyptic in character with the passing of time. Thus the earlier eschatology, which "envisages a definitive pattern of historical relationships," is gradually transformed into the dualistic view of history, which is "characterized by the end of the present aeon and the coming of the new aeon. . . ."[7]

To be sure, as Otto Plöger himself knows, this presentation of two clear fronts undoubtedly oversimplifies the complex intra-Jewish developments during the Persian and Greek eras. As soon as the sources begin to flow more freely, with the beginning of the Maccabean revolt, we recognize a multiplicity of related and conflicting manifestations of Jewish piety. However, in view of the scanty sources, the development conjectured by Otto Plöger can be demonstrated, generally speaking, only in its basic structure. But with due acknowledgment of its largely hypothetical character, it has more than a little historical probability in its favor.

In this connection, where we have to do with the

transition from the restorationist-historical eschatology of the prophets to the dualist-transcendent apocalyptic, the obvious thing is to recall the fact that in the apocalyptic literature it is not unusual for both conceptions to appear together. Frequently they are mingled in indistinct fashion, so that one can hardly discern which conception is dominant and which possesses only an auxiliary function. Moreover, it is often true, as for example in the Ethiopic Book of Enoch, that earlier literary strata with a more material-earthly eschatology are interlarded with later ones with a purely transcendental hope. Such intermingling in fact points to a process of transition from the restorationist eschatology of the prophets to the apocalyptic expectation of the new eon.

But, as we have already seen, apocalyptic itself is aware of the essential difference between the two patterns of thought, and thus we come to the question what, after all, the ingenious derivation of apocalyptic initiated by Otto Plöger is able to achieve for our comprehension of the phenomenon of "apocalyptic."

Apocalyptic clearly develops the view of the messianic interregnum which as an earthly kingdom at the end of time will last forty or four hundred or a thousand years, while the evil powers are bound. It is only thereafter that the final struggle with Satan begins, the dead arise, the judgment is held, this corrupt world collapses, and the new creation is manifested. This so-called chiliasm is found in like manner in both Jewish and Christian apocalyptic. It points to the fundamental difference between the prophetic and the apocalyptic hope and thus makes us aware of the limited value of all attempts to derive apocalyptic from the prophetic movement. Even in its later form, prophetic eschatology aims at the consummation of creation, at history's reaching its goal, at the conquest of evil by good; it envisages God's dealing with Israel in judgment and grace and the sanctifying activity of the Israelites which is made possible by God's action. It does not set its hopes on the world, it is true, but it has hope for the world.

Apocalyptic, on the other hand, despairs of history, gives up on creation, sharply separates good and evil, regards any commitment to this eon as senseless, and denies any prospect for man in history.

These two understandings of existence cannot be brought into agreement with each other. In their extreme formulation, they even stand in direct opposition to each other. Therefore they are really—that is, in what is distinctive and proper to each—not to be derived from each other, however positively one may assess the possibility of drawing a somewhat continuous line of development from prophecy to apocalyptic. Hence we cannot agree with Plöger when he asserts that prophetic eschatology *inevitably* had to change into the apocalyptic vision of the future as soon as the eschatological certainty of faith announced its claim anew in a theocratic community.[8] In the apocalyptic experience of existence what is involved is not just a "more severe and stringent version" of prophetic eschatology, but an essentially different and new understanding of historical reality in general. The "fundamental alteration and change"[9] of the old eschatological hope, as it takes place in apocalyptic, is not accounted for in terms of a mere acceptance and extension of the prophetic beginnings. The "new" in the apocalyptic experience of existence no more stems from prophetism than it does from Wisdom or from Iranian religion. Therefore it also does not represent the sum of these patterns of piety, even though apocalyptic is presented *objectively* as a combination of Old Testament–prophetic and Iranian elements with additions provided by the Wisdom movement.

This impossibility of deriving apocalyptic in the strict sense, in the "real" sense, from prophecy would not be dispelled even if we possessed more sources and could trace clearly the gradual and continuous transition from postexilic prophecy to apocalyptic hope. The apocalyptic experience of reality as such, which stands at the end of this process, would not thereby be moved closer to the Old Testament point of departure.

But this brings us to our next set of problems, namely, the question whether some characteristic political or social realities provoked the transformation of the prophetic understanding of existence into the apocalyptic one. Was it external circumstances, which by some inner necessity turned the lively eschatological interest that was present in certain circles of postexilic Judaism into that decline, that finally led to apocalyptic? Was it perhaps that in some particular historical situation disappointment over the fact that the eschatological hopes were not fulfilled broke out in such radical form that it led to a revolution from eschatological hope to apocalyptic expectation? Or did "the need to reconcile the utterances of the prophets with the actual state of affairs" in which Israel found itself in the Hellenistic period "exert a powerful effect"[10] in the emergence of apocalyptic, so that apologetic necessities, arising out of particular circumstances of the times, impelled the stewards of the prophetic legacy to the formation of apocalyptic ideas?

People have cited various circumstances and facts which are said to have led in this way to the annoyance and vexation with the world and the loss of a sense of history on the part of apocalyptic. In that respect it certainly is not sufficient to explain apocalyptic, as occasionally happens, as a Jewish defensive movement against the penetration of the Hellenistic spirit. Apocalyptic is far from being "reactionary" enough for that, and besides had long since outgrown the Old Testament–Jewish spirit far too much. Of course, anti-Hellenistic motives could also have played a part in the formation of apocalyptic, particularly since no Hellenist could muster any understanding for the apocalyptic view of the world and existence. But such motivations are not sufficient to account for the origin of apocalyptic.

As we have seen, Otto Plöger thinks of the opposition of the eschatological circles, the heirs of the later prophetic movement, to the established priestly aristocracy in the Persian period, and also supports his case with sociological arguments. He recalls, further, the collapse of the Persian empire, through which the eschatological hopes are said to have been revived about 300 B.C., and the schism of the Samaritans, which may very well have taken place at the same time and could have had an especially discouraging impact in those circles that had hoped for an eschatological renewal of all Israel.

Others point to the transfer of Palestine from the rule of the Ptolemies to the Seleucid authority soon after 200 B.C., and to the controversies that followed within Judaism between the conservative friends of Egypt and the followers of the Seleucids, who were responsive and open to Hellenism.

Still others concede a major role in the rise of apocalyptic to the suppression of the Jews by Antiochus

Epiphanes, to his attempt to transform Jerusalem into a Greek community, and to his desecration of the temple on Mount Zion. Indeed, the earliest extant apocalypse, the Book of Daniel, was actually written soon after the desecration of the temple (167), but before the death of Antiochus (163).

Many students of the matter also devote attention to the time of the Maccabean wars which began in 167 B.C. ("The time of the Maccabean struggles brought the greatest shocks to the stability of Judaism. Such times can be fruitful; new perceptions can mature in them"[11]), and one can then go further and seek, not the origin of apocalyptic in general, but the respective occasions for new literary activity, in political events such as the destruction of Jerusalem in the year A.D. 70 or the revolt under Bar Cochba (132–35). 4 Esdras unquestionably belongs to the approximate time of the Jewish catastrophe after 70.

Now of course there can be no doubt that there were "apocalyptic" situations, that is, times which were so filled with sorrow and destruction, turmoil and oppression, that eschatologically oriented groups saw no more hope at all for this world and concentrated their hopes entirely on a new, coming eon. It cannot be denied that such a political state of affairs could have furthered the development of the apocalyptic understanding of existence. Of course, the Maccabean wars come too late for an *initial development* of apocalyptic; for not even the Book of Daniel, which appeared shortly before that, marks the *origin* of apocalyptic. In it we see only the application of "what was already current to particular relationships and circumstances."[12] Besides, it is hardly likely that Judaism accepted the Iranian kind of piety, as heartily as is done in apocalyptic thought, for the first time in the Maccabean period, in which it shut itself off from all alien elements. For this reason it is difficult to point to a particular political situation which could have performed the service of midwife in the emergence of apocalyptic in the manner described; for the earlier period is, for us, concealed in an obscurity which can be illumined only by hypotheses.

To be sure, it has also been asserted that in the development of apocalyptic the political circumstances were of less significance than the social conditions. But unfortunately we have only very imperfect knowledge of the social and economic conditions in the centuries in question, and hardly anything certain can be determined even about the social structure of the original apocalyptic circles. Undoubtedly the circumstances of Israel in the Persian and Hellenistic periods were relatively impoverished. Nehemiah's chronicle (Neh. 5) tells of a great indebtedness of many plain people to the prominent Jews and of a general cancellation of debts which Nehemiah achieved. Of course, even the rich inhabitants appear not to have been able to lead a very luxurious life. Archaeology has brought to light nothing worthy of mention by way of cultural achievement from these centuries.

On the other hand, the foreign rulers appear not to have interfered with the matters of property in the country. Apparently we cannot speak of any economic exploitation. Of course, taxes had to be paid and officials had to be supported. Nehemiah is proud of having renounced his right to maintenance as governor (Neh. 5:14-19). Yet on the whole it appears that no very unusual social circumstances prevailed in the land of Palestine.

To be sure, there is a common and stereotyped polemic against the powerful, kings, the rich, and the lofty, especially in the parables of the Ethiopic Book of Enoch:

> Woe to those who build their houses by means of sin. (94:7)
>
> Woe to you rich. . . . (94:8)
>
> Woe to you who unjustly acquire silver and gold. . . . (97:8)
>
> Woe to you who build your houses by means of the toil of others, and whose building materials are nothing but bricks and stones of sin. . . . (99:13)

Yet these cries of woe are traditional in nature, as is shown by their harking back to Old Testament passages,[13] and they are not characteristic of apocalyptic alone, or even of apocalyptic at all. It would be incorrect to take them as a starting point and thus to make certain social grievances responsible for the emergence of apocalyptic. It is true that they show that the apocalyptic circles, as a whole, are composed of "plain people," who were without political and economic influence. Moreover, as is clearly evident from the Ethiopic Book of Enoch, these circles did not participate in the party struggles and political disputes within Judaism—this is in keeping with their pessimism with respect to this eon—and consequently found no protection and no justice with the ruling groups; for the latter "did not heed their cry and did not wish to listen to their voice. They helped those who robbed, devoured, and plundered them; they covered up their violence, and did not lift from them the yoke of those who devoured, destroyed, and murdered them. . . ."[14]

But we must not rely too heavily on such indications, especially since they all come, in fact, from relatively late sources. At any rate, it cannot be inferred from the texts that social problems played an essential role in the formation of the apocalyptic experience of reality, and the apocalyptic literature as such shows that among the apocalyptists there were also some people of more than a little culture and education.

Of course, it may be assumed that those groups which stood on the bright side of life generally showed little inclination to be open and receptive to apocalyptic thought. Anyone who enjoys the advantages of historical existence will hardly denounce history as such and will hardly be able totally to negate the existing state of affairs. Therefore one will certainly not go astray in characterizing apocalyptic piety as essentially a piety of the poor. In this way Luke 6:20-25 may very well reflect the apocalyptic understanding of existence of the time of Jesus, and in a Christian Sibylline oracle the greed for gold and silver is characterized as the source of all evil:

It is the source of godlessness and signpost to disorder,
Cause of all wars, abominable enemy of peace,
It makes the parents odious to the children and the children to the parents.
Without gold no marriage ever is honored.
And the land is given boundaries, and every sea its guards,
Craftily apportioned only to those who possess gold and treasures.
And if they should eternally possess the fruitful earth,
They will plunder the poor, so that they themselves will
Acquire still more land, and boastfully subject
it to themselves in a rage for greatness.[15]

But as surely as such passages are immediately comprehensible in an apocalyptic context and moreover may very well be characteristic to a large extent of apocalyptic piety, it is just as certain that the ancient sources do not permit us to hold particular social circumstances directly responsible for the emergence of apocalyptic. Besides, apocalyptic does not in any case understand itself to be a reaction to a particular social reality, and in view of our limited historical knowledge it remains questionable whether we may understand it thus.

The same also holds true for gnosis, which at about the same time gave expression to an understanding of existence which is akin to that of apocalyptic. To be sure, the gnostic texts betray even less of the social circumstances of their authors and readers than do the apocalyptic writings, though of course on the whole they suggest an aristocratic rather than a plebeian background. Hence it has been thought that the gnosis of antiquity arose as a reaction of a stratum of intellectuals to Rome's placing under her political tutelage the peoples of the East. Earthly power and dominion were experienced as coercion, and therefore were labeled as demonic and connected with supraterrestrial powers and dominions. In this way the cosmos organized in terms of such dominion in general was consigned to evil, and by means of a dualistic view the gnostic imagined himself in a relationship to God that was free from such dominion; he understood himself in essence as a part of the divine world of light which is superior to the cosmos.[16]

One could, then, think of apocalyptic as having arisen similarly, only in a stratum on a lower social level which does not deny lordship in general, but has the expectation that the evil earthly powers, which politically and socially oppress the nation of pious people, must yield to the good, peaceful, and helpful rule of God. In both cases, in this version then, people were raised as "knowing ones" or "righteous ones" out of the leveling mass of "subjects" to the freedom of "persons."

To be sure, in all these reflections we are dealing with pure hypotheses. But whatever their probability, at this point in our investigation the comparison with gnosis helps, in a quite different way, with a conclusive clarification of the question as to the origin of apocalyptic.

We have seen that essentially the same experience of reality is expressed in gnosis and apocalyptic. But it is also evident that, apart from some individual secondary influences, there were no direct historical connections between gnosis and apocalyptic. It is true that some have occasionally expressed the conjecture that gnosis arose out of apocalyptic; disappointment over the *new* eon's failure to appear at the end of time is said to have been transformed into the hope of the eon *above*. The sequence from prophetic eschatology to apocalyptic because of disappointed hopes was thus repeated in the step from apocalyptic to gnosis. But this conjecture cannot be correct. For there is no road that leads from the historical thinking of Jewish apocalyptic to the being-oriented thinking of gnosis, and actually such a connection of the two movements in a history of tradition cannot in any way be demonstrated. Apocalyptic and gnosis give expression to the same understanding of existence, but independently of each other and under totally different intellectual presuppositions.

But this also means that this understanding of existence in its "essential" meaning cannot actually be derived from prophetic eschatology. For it is beyond question that it does *not* occur in *gnosis* at the end of a line that originates in Old Testament prophecy. This may surely be asserted regardless of how one evaluates the attempts—in my opinion incorrect—otherwise to locate the roots of gnosis in Judaism. Thus in the last analysis the similar experience of existence, which gnosis and apocalyptic express independently of each other and in different fashion, cannot at all be traced out in terms of the history of a tradition.

This does not mean that we take back anything of what we have said about the connection of prophetic eschatology and apocalyptic. The assumption that the two phenomena are connected in a line of continuity has every probability in its favor. But the decline from post-exilic prophecy to apocalyptic, however it may have run in detail, was not an inevitable one implicit in the development itself. This decline must have been guided "from without," that is, by the changing understanding of reality itself. In other words, the apocalyptic experience of existence does not grow out of a process in the history of tradition, but arises without derivation out of the existential encounter with reality and then in its turn determines the development of the prophetic movement. Those people who with the help of primarily Iranian conceptual material reshaped the legacy of the last prophets to conform to their new basic experiences of reality *were already apocalyptists;* but apocalyptic did not arise when prophecy and Parseeism accidentally came into contact or when prophetic eschatology, in discussion with the theocracy or in view of its own failure, was *obliged* to undergo an "intensifying."

If it is true that the development from prophetic eschatology into apocalyptic hope was achieved "from without," we are of course faced once more with the question, finally, whether the new posture toward existence did not then just grow out of a new reality, and thus whether the question of origin cannot be definitively answered with the help of psychology and sociology, because certain realities inevitably produce a certain understanding of existence. The fact, already noted, that our sources do not provide adequate information about the political and social conditions during the time of the beginning of apocalyptic would then be a major handicap indeed, but still only a handicap with regard to needed material, which would only have the effect of hindering our following all the way to the end a methodologically correct and necessary insight.

But even if it is granted that apocalyptic is grounded in a specific, and in principle sociologically demonstrable, constellation of historical reality, still the apocalyptic attitude toward existence would remain and does remain lively outside this particular set of conditions also. Thus it can be detached from its presumed political and social presuppositions. It does not require on a continuing basis this sociological derivation or social rooting, for political and social changes have not extinguished the apocalyptic experience of existence. But this also means that the apocalyptic understanding of existence is proposed as a basic experience of existence for every possible derivation from the existing situation. It is always more than a reaction to causal structures in existing reality. It cannot die, because it was never born, and the fact that historical development cannot kill it shows that it was also not begotten by history, though it is certain of course that it does not live its life outside the boundaries of history.

This insight can be supported by the fact that in those times in which apocalyptic (as well as gnosis) was articulated, so far as we know no exceptionally frightful conditions prevailed which more than other times would have been bound to provoke pessimism, a loss of the sense of history, contempt for the world, and a hope of redemption. One can also point out that in any case apocalyptic represented only *one* reaction among various actual reactions, and that means that it was not an inevitable reaction to those presumed special circumstances of the time, as in every period the pressure of a harsh fate has also called forth a heightened will to live. Thus it must be seen that the "psychological" reaction to the historical situation is dependent upon a predisposition, and thus upon the at least potentially presupposed apocalyptic understanding of existence itself. One will also have to take into account the fact that, given a similar understanding of existence, apocalyptic and gnosis would hardly have arisen under the same political and social conditions.

Once again: Such considerations and reflections by no means contradict the intention to search out a real historical ground for the apocalyptic experience of existence in order to render it fruitful for the interpretation of apocalyptic. It is rather to be regretted that we know so little about the empirical native soil of the apocalyptic movement.

We must, however, be clear about the fact that even a complete clarification of the sociologically and psychologically comprehensible circumstances of the emergence of apocalyptic would not solve the question of origin in the sense of being a definitively and satisfactorily achieved statement of its derivation. This question of origin is explained prior to all attempts at derivation and in them, insofar as in the hopelessness of apocalyptic with respect to reality that can be experienced there is expressed a basic experience of existence which as such cannot be derived, that is, cannot be explained, but only affirmed or denied, accepted or rejected. To this extent the apocalyptic way of comprehending reality represents a particular experience of *faith*.

Rudolf Otto writes concerning apocalyptic dualism: "This removal of the world from the direct sphere of divine control has been traced back to the political conditions of late Judaism. There are no proofs. Rather it seems to me that the operative factor was an idea necessary to religion, and necessarily pressing its way more definitely into consciousness, viz. the idea of the transcendence of the divine over all that is of this world. It is the idea of the wholly other, the supramundane, which was first worked out in a mythical form in the contrasts between, and in the spatial superposition of, two spheres, that of earth and that of heaven."[17] It is true that the one does not rule out the other, and the dualism referred to is characteristic, not of religion *per se*, but of particular forms of religious experience. But Rudolf Otto has correctly seen that apocalyptic primarily has its roots within itself, namely in the apocalyptic experience of existence.

APOCALYPTIC AND CHRISTIANITY

In his book *Die jüdische Apokalyptik in ihrer geschichtlichen Entwicklung* [Jewish apocalyptic in its historical development] (1857), Adolf Hilgenfeld attempted to present evidence that apocalyptic forms the bridge from Old Testament Judaism to Christianity: ". . . how could anyone fail to see the most intimate and most direct connection between Jewish apocalyptic and the origin of Christianity. . . . Nothing else takes us so far into the actual birthplace of Christianity as does the pattern of thought of Jewish apocalyptic."[1]

Fifty years later, Albert Schweitzer, in his *Geschichte der Leben-Jesu-Forschung*,[2] pictures Jesus as an apocalyptist who is filled with ardent anticipation of the imminent end, who sends forth his disciples to announce the kingdom of God that is coming *now;* when, contrary to expectations, they return because the kingdom of God is not yet dawning, he makes his way to Jerusalem in the conviction that he must there seek out his painful death, in order thereby to focus upon himself the still-delayed time of the "messianic woes" and in this way to force the inbreaking of the kingdom of God.

Still another half-century later, Ernst Käsemann has set in motion a vigorous discussion with the assertion that apocalyptic is the mother of Christian theology, because even though Jesus himself did not do so, the Palestinian primitive community allowed itself in its interpretation of the Jesus-event to be wholly determined by apocalyptic.[3]

Whenever and with whatever modifications this thesis of the apocalyptic origin of Christianity has appeared, it has found vigorous opponents and equally convinced champions, and the problem which is posed along with it, that of the connection between apocalyptic and Christianity, is still a controversial one. It cannot be our task here to set forth this problem in detail and in all its nuances and divisions, particularly since an insight into the historical development of the inquiry is rendered extremely difficult by the fact that the *concept* of apocalyptic as used by the various students of the matter differs widely from case to case. We can only attempt, in connection with the previously gained understanding of apocalyptic and on the basis of our own insight into the nature of New Testament Christianity, to describe the relationship of the primitive Christian faith to apocalyptic piety in its basic features.

In so doing, one will make a distinction between the historical and the substantive relationship of the two religious currents to each other and, with respect to the substantive relationship, take into account a possible difference between the preaching of Jesus and the post-Easter belief in Jesus and to this extent, where applicable, apply a different definition of the substantive relationship.

Historical connections between Jesus and apocalyptic cannot be denied. It is certain that Jesus let himself be baptized by John, and the latter's baptism was a baptism of repentance with reference to the *now* coming kingdom of God. The primary and fundamental utterance of the community that looked back upon Jesus' activity was "He is risen," and this confession shows with sufficient clarity that the expectation of the resurrection of the dead as a *now* imminent eschatological act must have been an essential object of hope of the disciples who followed Jesus during his time on earth. Thus Jesus' appearance is bracketed as closely as possible by two fundamentally apocalyptic phenomena—the eschatological baptism of repentance and the Easter confession—and therefore it is not surprising that the words of Jesus that are handed down are not seldom rooted in the apocalyptic context.

There we meet the Son of Man as the coming judge of the world who is to be expected soon (Mark 14:62). On the other hand, Jesus sees Satan falling from heaven like lightning, that is, being cast out of his rule over the world (Luke 10:18). Numerous parables inculcate vigilance in view of the *now* coming kingdom of God (Matt. 12:39-40) and urge people for the sake of the one thing now needful to let all else go, to abandon the old eon for the sake of the new (Matt. 13:44-46). The call to sinners to repent is issued in view of the imminent judgment of the world (Matt. 4:17). The terrors of the end-time are portrayed, and warnings are issued against false messianic figures (Mark 13). One should observe and heed

the signs of the times—that is to say, of the end-time—
(Matt. 16:3); for "this generation" will not pass away
before the course of the old world-age is completed
(Mark 9:1). The conception of the kingdom of God of this
immediate expectation, however, is thoroughly
apocalyptic: it will come suddenly from beyond this
world and will appear everywhere at the same time, as a
flash of lightning shines from one end of the heavens to
the other (Matt. 24:27).

Of course, the Jesus-tradition is also acquainted with
utterances which apparently do not allow us simply to
classify Jesus, even as to the substance of the matter,
with the apocalyptic movement. To be sure, in view of
the Palestinian setting of his proclamation, the fact that
in his proclamation universalistic utterances appear to
be lacking says nothing. Moreover, the apocalyptic
character of Jesus' preaching is not contradicted by the
fact that there is no tradition of an outline of history from
his lips whereby his own present time is identified as the
end-time; for such surveys are by no means indispensable to apocalyptic, and besides, they make sense only in
pseudonymous writings. But in the ancient sayings-
tradition we encounter extended paraenetic passages;
one may think, for example, of the Sermon on the
Mount. According to Albert Schweitzer, who presents
Jesus in extreme fashion as an apocalyptist, this material
served as foundation for an interim ethic, that is, as
guidance for the ordering of life during the short time
before the end of the world—a very problematical pro-
posal, for this sayings-material does not represent itself
as pertaining to an interim, nor do we find a comparable
interim ethic elsewhere in the realm of apocalyptic.

The Jesus-tradition also exhibits, in many of its parts,

an extremely close relationship to this creation; one
should think again of the Sermon on the Mount and its
words about the lilies of the field and the fowls of the air.
So did Jesus break with apocalyptic piety at the crucial
point? Was his own course in conflict, as Ernst
Käsemann asserts,[4] with his beginnings in the circle
around the Baptist? Did he call man to daily service of
God "as if no shadows lay upon the world and God were
not inaccessible"? Käsemann is convinced that "it is just
the historian who is obliged to speak of a unique secret in
Jesus," of the remarkable historical phenomenon of an
"escape" of Jesus from the previously given apocalyptic
thought.

Nevertheless this explanation is not satisfactory, because earliest Christianity maintains its connection with
Jesus primarily by means of the explicit apocalyptic confession of the resurrection of the dead that has arrived.
Is this supposed to have happened in conflict with the
intentions of Jesus' preaching? But on the other hand,
one cannot easily make a total separation, in terms of the
history of tradition, between the apocalyptic and the
nonapocalyptic portions of the Jesus-tradition and at-
tribute the latter exclusively to the later community. To
be sure, I am most inclined toward this solution of the
problem, without intending thereby to assume for Jesus
an extreme attitude of rejection of the world and of
history. For even though, because of the problems about
its authenticity, our Jesus-tradition provides no certain
historical information, still the theology of early Christianity hardly allows the conclusion that the inbreaking
kingdom of God had for Jesus no connection with history.

It seems as though Jesus—like John the Baptist before him, in the context of apocalyptic, indeed, but with a

significant modification of what is common to apocalyptic—was interested in the announcement of the end, not for the sake of the end itself and its consequences, but because of the chance that was opened up in this last hour for the poor and sinners to participate in the coming salvation. Characteristic of him, therefore, was the *invitation* into the coming kingdom, the call to repentance as the way open to all into the kingdom of God, and the *offer* of the dawning salvation for the whole world. It is understandable that from the very beginning this proclamation was bound up with instructions in a love-ethic for the circle of the pious ones and that sooner or later it could be combined with comforting glimpses, originating in the Wisdom tradition, into the beneficent rule of God in creation.

But what is *really* evident is in principle only the fact that all attempts to gain from our tradition a picture of the historical Jesus do not go beyond assailable hypotheses and disputed probabilities. This state of affairs is based primarily on the fact that from the very beginning the Christian church did not confess the so-called historical Jesus, but Jesus as the crucified and resurrected one. The confessional formulas of the primitive community take no notice of the teaching, life, deeds, and conduct of Jesus, but testify to his incarnation, his death, his resurrection, and his exaltation as the event of divine salvation. This "kerygmatic" Jesus provides the basis of the Christian understanding of existence. Insofar as a "historical" Jesus-tradition occurs at all—outside the Synoptic Gospels it admittedly is almost totally lacking—it does not provide the basis of the confession, but is intended to be read and interpreted in the light of the confession.

Therefore the question as to the substantive relationship of the apocalyptic and Christian ways of understanding existence is not the same as the problem of the connections of *Jesus* with apocalyptic. The obvious impossibility of giving a satisfactory explanation for this latter problem on the basis of the early Christian sources helps us properly to pose our primary question. This is the question as to the relationship of apocalyptic, not to the "historical" Jesus who stands behind the New Testament tradition, but to this tradition itself as the immediate expression of the Christian belief in Jesus, the crucified and risen Lord of his community and of the world.

But then there follows a fundamental *historical* connection with apocalyptic through the confession of the resurrection of Jesus; for this confession stands at the beginning of the Christian kerygma. Easter is the foundational datum of the Christian church.

However, one can read in this datum the most important element in the *substantive* relationship of the apocalyptic and the Christian experience of existence. That is to say, the resurrection of Jesus was originally interpreted as the beginning of the general resurrection of the dead. According to Paul in 1 Cor. 15:20, Jesus arose as the "first fruits of those who have died." Thus Jesus' resurrection signals the onset of the end-events; it introduces the time of judgment and the inbreaking of the new eon. The community which was gathered around the confession of the resurrected Jesus accordingly understood itself as the community of salvation. Whatever one may ascertain by way of developments in the theology of the primitive community and early Christianity, in all the variations of primitive Christian theology this basic idea is unfolded: Christian theology understands the historical event "Jesus Christ" as eschatological event, sees God acting definitively for the salvation of the world in the cross and resurrection of Jesus, and regards Christian existence in this world as existence in the dawning eschatological kingdom of God. Salvation therefore appears in the Christian proclamation, in contrast to apocalyptic, as a historical possibility and, where this possibility is seized, as present historical reality.

Viewed historically, the relationship of apocalyptic and Christianity is that of expectation and fulfillment, and insofar as Jesus must in essence be described as an apocalyptist, the religion of Jesus also is substantively related to the belief in Jesus as the hope of God's saving action is related to the confession of God's saving deed. Hence it must be regarded as appropriate that the primitive Christian church did not make the "historical" Jesus, that is, the stage of anticipation, the object of its theology.

Of course, this "now, already" of salvation must not be misunderstood in the gnostic sense, as happened in heretical circles of early Christianity. For salvation is not a possession at the disposal of the community, but is promised to her out of grace. Christians are saved in hope. The community of salvation may at any given time live by God's promise that he is with her and that her salvation consists in that fact. Thus this salvation does not lie in the near or distant future, but in the ever-present futurity of God, and it is actualized where man abandons himself as the basis of life and ventures to live out of the promise of grace which sets him free from the state of being a victim of his past and from anxiety about his future, to live life at every moment in love and hope. To this extent the "now, already" of Christian salvation can properly be understood only in connection with the "not yet," and this connection must be conceived dialectically, not quantitatively: salvation is already wholly present and yet is still wholly outstanding; it is unconditionally present and at the same time wholly future. For it is *God's* salvation which as such is entirely endowed with actuality wherever man yields with his life to God's coming in Christ, and which at the same time never becomes his possession, because he can only await it ever anew.

Insofar as the dramatic conceptions of the apocalyptic end-history or of the end of history are maintained in the early Christian proclamation—and except for the Johannine literature, this happens throughout—these traditional ideas therefore have the primary function of warning against a gnosticizing misinterpretation of the salvation-event and of insuring the dialectical understanding of salvation as a gift of grace which is not at man's disposal. Thus the temporal coefficient of the apocalyptic expectation loses its dominant function; the anticipation of the imminent end of the world, which originally was dominant among Jesus' disciples, can in the course of time be abandoned without a fundamental crisis. People soon come to emphasize that one cannot know the time of the end, but must hold oneself in readiness at all times. The expectation of the return of Christ and the judgment of the world that is connected with it also dissolves the apocalyptic understanding of existence, because the coming Lord is none other than the present Lord of history, who causes his servants to live historically in the kingdom of his liberty.

Correspondingly, the Christian relationship to history must also be understood dialectically. Anyone who asks about the *place* of salvation is pointed by the Christian proclamation to history, so certainly is the Christ-event as salvation-event historically achieved. Thus the loss of the sense of history that is characteristic of apocalyptic has no place in the Christian kerygma. But it is also true that salvation is not expected from history itself, but from God. It enters into history from beyond history. To this extent the apocalyptic dualism is maintained. Man can only *receive* salvation, and he receives it in his historical place. But he cannot out of his own historical possibilities give form in a saving way to the world that is devoid of salvation; for he himself needs redemption from ruin—not from the ruin of history, as is the case in apocalyptic, but from his own lost condition, that is, from ruin *in* history, into which God has entered through Jesus Christ and thus has brought salvation to men by robbing the "God of this eon" of his power and disclosing himself to men historically as the source of man's life.

The apocalyptic dualism whose schema is preserved in the New Testament proclamation in the way described, logically and consistently loses its cosmic determinism and becomes a dualism of decision. The old and new eons do not stand opposed as mutually exclusive in temporal terms, but overlap in the midst of history. For the believer Christ signifies the end of the old world-age in time, and for the nonbeliever condemnation in the midst of temporality. The apocalyptic waiting for the end of this world-age is transformed into the historical decision for the heavenly kingdom of liberty and peace, truth and love, *in* which the love of God allows the Christian to live—in the face of death.

This substantive relationship of apocalyptic and New Testament is indeed represented in different ways in the various New Testament writings according to the historical situation and the respective backgrounds of the various writers, but it is always set forth as the same relationship.

Thus we read in Paul, for example, with repeated use and corresponding adaptation of the apocalyptic terminology:

> If anyone is in Christ, he is a "new creation"; the old has passed away, and behold, the new has come to be. (2 Cor. 5:17)

A little later he quotes Isaiah 49:8:

> At the acceptable time I heard you,
> And on the day of salvation I helped you,

and then adds:

> Behold, now is the most acceptable time; behold, now is the day of salvation. (2 Cor. 6:2)

Thus the present stands under the sign of the time which has come to fulfillment; for

> when the time was fulfilled, God sent his Son, born of a woman, . . . so that we might receive the status of children. (Gal. 4:4-5)

Luther, following the train of Pauline theology, appropriately interprets this sentence, not to mean that Christ came when the established time of the old eon had run its course, but that with the coming of Christ the old eon comes to an end.

The apocalyptic blessings hoped for are accordingly present gifts of salvation: "The kingdom of God consists in . . . righteousness and peace and joy in the Holy Spirit" (Rom. 14:17).

For the Christians there is no more condemnation (Rom. 8:1); for "because we have been pronounced righteous by faith, we have peace with God through our Lord Jesus Christ" (Rom. 5:1).

In the most forthright apocalyptic language Paul can speak of the devil as the god of this world-age (2 Cor. 4:4) and of the demonic powers as the rulers of this eon (1 Cor. 2:9), but for him they are also already disarmed in Christ (Rom. 8:38-39). God has "disarmed the principalities and powers and made a public display of them" when he installed Christ in his glory (Col. 2:15). Therefore Paul can appeal to the church "by the mercies of God" not to be conformed to "this eon," but—as citizens of the kingdom of God that has dawned in Christ—to be transformed by the renewing of the mind, that is, in keeping with the new eon (Rom. 12:1-2).

To be sure, Paul has no doubt that "the form of this cosmos is passing away" (1 Cor. 7:31), but this awareness does not lead to a contempt for history, in which in fact the new eon has already dawned, but to a denial of the possibility of living *on the resources* of this dying world. Faith brings into the world the possibility of eschatological existence in the midst of this world, and the basic insistence that we walk by the Spirit, as well as the manifold concrete admonitions to a corresponding conduct, shows how little the protest against this eon as the *basis* of life signifies a contempt for historical life in general. The current accusation against Christianity that it abstains from changing the historical situation therefore does not apply to Paul—and moreover, not to the history of the church as a whole. It has validity only if the demand for transformation of the world is propounded from the perspective of the apocalyptic utopia and—contrary to the dualistic eon-thought of apocalyptic—is posed in this form to *the* man who has brought about the present state of the world. For in the New Testament, in fact, the function of the redeemer is never attributed to autonomous man. Both Christianity and apocalyptic reckon with "sin" as a force which man cannot overcome by his own powers; for Paul, man is himself a sinner, and as such cannot free himself from himself. He requires liberation from his sinful longing for autonomy, and this "conversion" of man is the prerequisite for any change in the world.

This "eschatological reserve," that is, the confession that new life is always a life bestowed out of grace, is served by the apocalyptic passages which, not by accident, occur in Paul's writings, primarily in his debate with the gnostics.[5] Over against those who glory in their own wisdom, their inalienable *possession* of salvation, their inner Christ, in short, in *themselves*, Paul emphasizes that he indeed has been apprehended by Christ, but by no means has himself perfectly apprehended (Phil. 3:12); that the creation still sighs in the expectation of the revelation of the "sons of God" (Rom. 8:19); and that we walk by faith and not by sight (2 Cor. 5:7)—without thereby annulling the triumphant cry of the new man in the new eon: "Death is swallowed up in victory; O death, where is your victory? Death, where is your sting?" (1 Cor. 15:55). Similarly, the passage 1 Cor. 15:1 ff., thoroughly marked by apocalyptic, ends with the sentence "But thanks be to God, who gives us the victory through our Lord Jesus Christ" (15:57 RSV), which Luther quite properly interpreted as ". . . who has given us the victory."

Thus it may be said that the apocalyptic motifs in Paul serve for the explication of the doctrine of justification. They guard the message of the already accomplished justification of the sinner against sliding into an assurance of existence which no longer requires the elements of hope and faith.

The predominantly Jewish-Christian tradition before and contemporary with Paul is expressed in language and a set of concepts essentially different from those of the apostle to the Gentiles, but in the crucial points it gives expression to the same understanding of the world and of existence.

The present and the future of the Lord, the "now, already" and the "not yet" of salvation are dialectically intertwined with each other. For the present Lord of the community is expected as the coming Lord, and the salvation already bestowed is viewed as eternal: "Lo, I am with you always, to the end of the age"—the Gospel of Matthew closes with these words (28:20), that is, with a promise of salvation which deliberately rejects all apocalyptic interest in the date of the end of the world, because for the Christian the new eon has dawned already under the lordship of Christ.

John reflects in an especially intensive way upon the relationship of the Christian faith to apocalyptic's understanding of existence, which to be sure he has in view, not primarily in its Jewish-apocalyptic form, but in its gnostic form. But we have seen that apocalyptic and gnosis give expression to the same experience of existence in quite diverse patterns of thought. Therefore an anti-gnostic theology implies a criticism also of apocalyptic.

John describes the status of the believer as living in the light: "The darkness is passing away and the true light is already shining" (1 John 2:8 RSV). Anyone who takes his stand on Jesus' side has passed through the eschatological judgment and won life; he already has death behind him: "Truly, truly, I say to you, whoever hears my word and believes the one who sent me, has eternal life and will not come into judgment, but has passed from death into life" (John 5:24-25), and "I am the resurrection and the life. Whoever believes in me will live, even if he were dead; and everyone who lives and believes in me will never die" (John 11:25-26).

Correspondingly, the apocalyptic blessings of salvation of the end-time are present reality:

the truth—for the believers practice the truth (John 3:21);

liberty—for "if the Son shall make you free, you shall be free indeed" (John 8:36);

peace—for Jesus gives peace to those who are his own, not a merely apparent peace, which the world gives (John 14:27);

the disarming of the "princes of this world"—for the believers are taken up into the victory of Christ over evil (1 John 2:13);

joy—which for the disciples is characterized as "complete" and thus is described as eschatological (John 16:24; 17:13).

But if life is presently, historically actualized as an eschatological gift, John can reject the apocalyptic or gnostic protest against history as such. He does this with

Christological sentences such as "The word became flesh" (John 1:14), or "God so loved the cosmos that he gave his only Son . . ." (John 3:16). With reference to the community he has Jesus praying, "I do not ask that you should take them out of the world, but that you should preserve them from the evil one" (John 17:15). Thus for the believer Satan has lost his power over this cosmos, and God has assumed his lordship. The new world is the old creation that has been made new by God.

Therewith the old commandment of love comes into effect anew in the community, so that it can appear as a new commandment (1 John 2:7-8); for in the eschatological existence the commandment of love can finally be realized; faith liberates man from concern about himself and thus sets him free for service to his neighbor. Therefore the believer experiences the actuality of the new eon in the fulfillment of the commandment of love: "We know that we have passed from death into life; for we love the brethren" (1 John 3:14). Therewith the *historical* dimension of the "new eon" as a present eon finds especially pregnant expression.

John deliberately refers to the form of expression of apocalyptic-gnostic dualism when he makes it plain that man presently stands at the point of decision between life and death, salvation and perdition, light and darkness. But he radically denies the history-rejecting foundation of the dualistic eon-thought; for salvation and perdition alike are historical realities. It is true that the community does not live *by* this world, but she does live *in* it. She is at home here, because God has once again made the world his own property, and she sojourns in a foreign land only insofar as the world has turned away from God.

John after all consistently refrains from handing on apocalyptic conceptions and images of apocalyptic hopes. This fact discloses how high a level of reflection his theology has attained. To be sure, it has occasionally exposed him to the accusation that he is on the way to a gnostic enthusiasm and is on the verge of abandoning the *extra nos* of salvation and thus the reserve about eschatology as well. This feeling apparently prevailed even when his work was issued at the beginning of the second century; for it may very well have been at that time that those passages were inserted which, in obvious tension with their context, represent an apocalyptic expectation of the future: John 5:28-29; 6:39-40, 44; (12:48).

But with such criticism as this, one will hardly be doing justice to John. He is not thinking of abandoning his reservations with respect to eschatology. He only regards the apocalyptic way of thinking as not very well suited for impressing upon his readers the "not yet" along with the "now, already." Apparently he fears that in this way the dialectic of any future salvation could degenerate into a quantitative classification of the blessings of salvation, of which part are already bestowed and part are yet to come. Therefore he provides a place for his reservation about eschatology, which in his view cannot be surrendered. He does this primarily by explicitly impressing upon his readers the "cosmos" and the "sarx" (world and flesh: 1:14; 3:16), that is, this hopeless history, as the place, the locus, of the *eschatological* salvation, so that salvation can only be encountered now and again from beyond this history. In other words, it can be experienced historically, but is never historically accessible. He also never wearies of stressing the necessity of *remaining* with Christ or "in Christ."

The nonapocalyptic train of primitive Christian thought is also exhibited in thoroughgoing fashion in the fact that it is not apocalypses but the gospel and the letter or epistle that determine the form of early Christian literature. Only the "Apocalypse of John" forms an exception to this rule among the New Testament writings.

A theological puzzle, even more than a historical one, is contained in the fact that the sole independent apocalypse that was accepted into the New Testament has been attributed to the same author as the only complex of New Testament writings that completely excludes the apocalyptic motifs, namely, the Gospel and the Epistles of John.

Already in antiquity well-founded doubts were expressed about the conviction that the Apocalypse came from the same author as the other Johannine writings. The assumption of identical authorship in fact can in no way be maintained.

To be sure, one will hardly be doing the "Revelation of John" justice by simply classifying this book as apocalyptic. The very fact that it was not written anonymously, but gives the name of its author and the place of its contemporary emergence, should warn us against such an evaluation. Besides, the book contains two clear complexes of contemporary relevance: In the seven "Letters" at the beginning of the book a warning against the gnostic heresy, and in all its passages an intensive word of comfort in the face of governmental persecutions. Accordingly, one must ask whether the "apocalyptic" aspect of this last book of the Bible is not to be understood in terms of the direct connection with these current problems of the church of the "seer" John. For because the overpowering of the anti-Christian power of the state with its idolatrous emperor-cult is conceived by John as a part of the apocalyptic drama of the end, the apocalyptic schema helps the community to understand its present situation as meaningful. And in that history becomes meaningful in this way as the place of the present contest with the power of evil, the author of Revelation at the same time refutes the gnostic enthusiasm which is interested only in the liberation of the Pneuma from its entanglement in worldly history, behaves in a libertine fashion in the certainty of pneumatic salvation, holds creation in contempt, and rejects constant penitence. Over against this enthusiasm, the traditional apocalyptic materials in the Book of Revelation tie the eschatological events to history, without thereby adopting the apocalyptic understanding of existence at all.

It must not be overlooked that, for the seer John, Christ is already enthroned in his rule and the songs of praise of the celestial and terrestrial creation echo the praise that is already being voiced in the Christian community:

To him who sits upon the throne and to the Lamb be blessing and honor and glory and might for ever and ever! (Rev. 5:13 RSV)

We give thanks to thee, Lord God Almighty, who art and who wast,
that thou hast taken thy great power and begun to reign. (11:17 RSV)

Now the salvation and the power and the kingdom of our God and the authority of his Christ have come, for the accuser of our brethren has been thrown down, who accuses them day and night before our God. (12:10 RSV)

Hallelujah! For the Lord our God the Almighty reigns.
Let us rejoice and exult and give him the glory,
for the marriage of the Lamb has come,
and his Bride has made herself ready. (19:6-7 RSV)

So even in the present the invitation to salvation is issued: "Let him who is thirsty come, let him who desires take the water of life without price" (22:17 RSV).

If this interpretation of the "Revelation" is correct, then its author is by no means reverting to unmodified apocalyptic, but in a strongly apocalyptic framework which exhibits many elements of the apocalyptic conceptual world is holding firm to the Christian interpretation of reality, which interprets the Christ-event as salvation-event and views the present as the time of salvation. Then the long-contested acceptance of the Apocalypse of John into the canon of the Christian church was not a blunder, as Luther, among others, thought in view of the misuse which the "Schwärmer" [i. e., fanatics] practiced with the book. Further, the understanding of what is Christian in the Revelation of John would then be less remote from the ideas of the other Johannine literature than is often assumed, even though the acceptance of a common authorship remains excluded by the essentially different character of the two bodies of literature.

Now, to be sure, the judgment concerning the Revelation of John, however it turns out, cannot decide the matter of the relationship of apocalyptic and the Christian faith; for in no case are we dealing with a *typically* Christian writing in the Apocalypse of John.

If we look at the whole of the early Christian tradition, then the relationship of Christianity and apocalyptic is undoubtedly grounded in a close *historical* connection between the two movements. This is shown both by the positive incorporation of apocalyptic thought-material into the early Christian traditions and by the critical discussion with the apocalyptic understanding of existence. For this reason we cannot totally deny the correctness of the thesis that apocalyptic was the mother of Christian theology, insofar as the *historical* relationship is in question. With respect to the *substantive* relationship, however, this assertion is by no means correct. For in substance the New Testament understanding of existence stands in sharp tension with the apocalyptic view of reality and relatively close to the original Old Testament declaration of the relationship of God, world, and man. For the Old Testament also confesses God's historical saving activity, which allows man in the midst of his world to experience, grasp, and hope for his salvation from God in such a way that the believer knows himself in the present to be a member of the people of God and can open himself to the call of God always to make his way out of all earthly securities into the future of God, just as Abraham left his father's house.

Therefore one can only label the fact that the really apocalyptic literature as such was accepted neither into the Jewish nor into the Christian canon as an appropriate theological decision.

MESSIAH AND SON OF MAN

We propose now to test the conclusions reached up to this point and our insights into apocalyptic thought and belief on a specific problem which for various reasons merits special interest and has often been the subject of penetrating study: the significance of the figure of the Messiah.

Every eschatological movement in the realm of Judaism must take up the problem of the Messiah. For in the Old Testament, which is normative for all Jews, eschatological hopes are frequently connected with the expectation of an eschatological ruler, the king from David's race. This expectation is connected with the early prophecy which Nathan communicated to David: "And your house and your kingdom shall be made sure for ever before me; your throne shall be established for ever" (2 Sam. 7:16 RSV).

Especially well-known advance announcements of the Messiah are found in Micah 5:1 ff.; Amos 9:11-12; and Isaiah 9:5-6.

172

In Zech. 4:14, alongside the descendant of David, Zerubbabel, who as Persian administrator exercises his office in Jerusalem and on whom the prophet Zechariah concentrates the messianic hopes, there stands in the high priest Joshua a second anointed one of Zadokite-priestly origin. In the period of the Israelite theocracy during the Persian and Syrian occupations, such a priestly Messiah even occupies the leading position in the context of the messianic expectation. In the post–Old Testament period, moreover, we find a Messiah from the house of Joseph or of Ephraim as representative of the former Northern kingdom.

Can a political king, who in the time of salvation once again restores the political ascendancy which Israel had achieved under David, play a role in apocalyptic?

This question must be answered without qualification in the negative. For the hope of the apocalyptists is directed precisely *against* a particularistic-national, politically based, and militarily secured expectation of salvation. The Davidic messianology reckons on a restitution in this eon of the lofty age which Israel had experienced, a restoration of the historical climax of Israelite history. The hope of the Davidic Messiah can be understood and maintained only in the form of an intrahistorical hope, that is, in the confidence that *history* is the place of the divine saving activity. Since such an expectation is in total contradiction to the apocalyptic understanding of history, apocalyptic could do nothing with the Messiah from the house of David or the political high priest from the house of Aaron.

Actually, therefore, *this* Messiah is totally lacking in the apocalyptic writings also. This absence is repeated moreover in the first century A.D., in the work of Philo, the famous Jewish theologian from Alexandria, who spiritualizes the Jewish eschatology. Of course, it is also to be observed in Jewish gnosis, which, because it is unable to speak of an end-time in this world, must also reject the figure of the Davidic Messiah.

To be sure, the figure of the Messiah does not remain altogether alien to apocalyptic literature.

Already in the Old Testament we occasionally encounter a transcendentalizing of the messianic hope: the Messiah bears features of the king of Paradise, and the messianic age is regarded as the age of Paradise which has returned.

Such mythical traces are perhaps already found in the blessing of Jacob upon Judah in Gen. 49:11-12, where according to the text which we read today it is said of the ruler from Judah:

> Binding his foal to the vine
>   and his ass's colt to the choice vine,
> he washes his garments in wine
>   and his vesture in the blood of grapes;
> his eyes shall be red with wine,
>   and his teeth white with milk. (RSV)

But in any case we find in Isaiah 11:6-9*a* the idea of Paradise. When the shoot shall have grown up out of the stump of Jesse, the father of David, then

> The wolf shall dwell with the lamb,
>   and the leopard shall lie down with the kid,
> and the calf and the lion and the fatling together,
>   and a little child shall lead them.
> The cow and the bear shall feed;
>   their young shall lie down together;
>   and the lion shall eat straw like the ox.

The sucking child shall play over the hole of the asp,
  and the weaned child shall put his hand on the adder's
    den.
They shall not hurt or destroy
  in all my holy mountain. (RSV)

Such ideas and images are incorporated and further expanded in the later Jewish eschatology, undoubtedly in constant exchange with the widely disseminated myth of the blessed end-time which leads back to the golden beginning.

Outside the Jewish-Christian sphere the Fourth Eclogue of Virgil offers the best-known example of this idea.

Corresponding views also occur in Iranian eschatology. Here the redeemer, who brings the world back to its original state of blessedness by definitively expelling from it the influence of the evil power, is called Saosyant, a divinely begotten human being like the Messiah, a victorious bearer of salvation.

In the Syriac Book of Baruch we read:

... the Messiah shall then begin to be revealed. ... The earth also shall yield its fruit ten thousandfold, and on one vine there shall be a thousand branches, and each branch shall produce a thousand clusters, and each cluster shall produce a thousand grapes, and each grape shall produce a cor of wine. And those who have hungered shall rejoice; moreover, also, they shall behold marvels every day. For winds shall go forth from Me to bring every morning the fragrance of aromatic fruits, and at the close of the day clouds distilling the dew of health. And it shall come to pass at that self-same time that the treasury of manna shall again descend from on high, and they shall eat of it in those years, because these are they who have come to the consummation of time.[1]

In the Testament of Levi 18, and thus also in the context of apocalyptic piety, there appears from among the descendants of Levi a *priestly* Messiah who in the paradisiacal end-time rules as king: "He himself shall open the doors of Paradise, take away the sword which threatened Adam, and give to the saints to eat of the tree of life."

Within Judaism such utopian representations of the end-time—whether with or without a messianic figure—occur particularly often, though not exclusively, in the apocalyptic literature, and accordingly they can easily be combined with the picture formed by apocalyptic hope. This becomes especially comprehensible in the light of two observations.

In the first place, this picture of utopian hope explodes the possibilities in real history. *This* end-time is purely the work of God. The notion that sinful man could, by concentrated commitment of his moral powers, bring about such a time of salvation is impossible. Even though it occurs *in* history, it marks the extreme periphery of history, that area in which this eon and that one meet. This state of affairs is very finely described in the Syriac Book of Baruch: "For that time is the consummation of that which is corruptible, and the beginning of that which is not corruptible. . . . Therefore it is far away from evils, and near to those things which die not."[2] Thus the figure of the dawn applies to this paradisiacal end-time: the night is already disappearing, and the day is no longer distant (cf. Rom. 13:11 ff.). In it we have to do with an impossible historical possibility, a genuine historical utopia.

Therefore in another context the same mythical portrayal of Paradise can also stand for an event whose actualization can in no way be anticipated. In the Book of Jubilees Esau declares to Jacob:

> When the wolves make peace with the lambs, that they will no longer devour them, and no more do them harm, and when their hearts will nothing but good for them, then there will be peace in my heart toward you.
>
> When the lion becomes a friend of the ox, and submits to *one* yoke with him and plows with him, then will I also make peace with you.[3]

From this Jacob rightly concludes that Esau "intends evil toward him in his heart." What Esau sets as a condition for reconciliation with his brother will never happen; hence with this condition Esau is rejecting any historical understanding with his brother.

Thus that end-time, where it appears as a "real" utopia, introduces into history a new quality; it is the historical possibility that has been *forfeited* by man, the age of Paradise, which only God can restore. Hence we can understand that the apocalyptic understanding of reality was in principle open to this mythical thought, for the nugatory Present of this present eon sharply contrasts with these utopias.

But the second observation is especially characteristic of the distinctive apocalyptic understanding of existence. The messianic kingdom portrayed in such utopian forms still belongs to *this* eon, even though it marks its outermost limits; it is part of the world that is passing away, whose intended but never yet realized actuality it sets forth. Thus we have to do with a messianic interregnum or the messianic kingdom of the end-time.

Therefore even the Messiah himself is a figure of this world-age. According to the Syriac Book of Baruch, he will rule in the blessed end-kingdom of history, "until the world of corruption is at an end, and until the times aforesaid are fulfilled."[4] Correspondingly, in 4 Esdras we read:

> For behold the days come, and it shall be when the signs
>   which I have foretold unto thee shall come to pass,
> [then shall the city that now is invisible appear,
> And the land which is now concealed be seen].
> And whoever is delivered from the predicted evils, the
>   same shall see my wonders. For my Son the Messiah
>   shall be revealed, together with those who are with
>   him, and shall rejoice the survivors four hundred years.
>   And it shall be, after these years, that my Son the
>   Messiah shall die and all in whom there is human
>   breath. Then shall the world be turned into the
>   primaeval silence seven days, like as in the first begin-
>   nings, so that no man is left. And it shall be after seven
>   days that the Age which is not yet awake, shall be
>   roused, and that which is corruptible shall perish.[5]

Then the dead arise, and then begins the judgment of the Most High. The few who are saved receive the life of the new world, which no eye has seen and no tongue can describe. We read similar statements in Syriac Baruch 30 and in 4 Esdras 11:46 or 12:31 ff.

The Antichrist, who rises against that Messiah of the end-time and is conquered by him, therefore appears likewise in the form of an earthly ruler, even though he may also be understood as historical manifestation of the superhuman Belial. We may compare, for example, Syriac Baruch 40:3 (Charles):

The last leader of that time shall be left alive, when the
multitude of his hosts shall be put to the sword, and he
shall be bound, and they shall take him up to Mount Zion,
and My Messiah shall convict him of all his impieties, and
shall gather and set before him all the works of his hosts.
And afterwards he shall put him to death, and protect the
rest of My people which shall be found in the place which I
have chosen,

that is, so long as the blessed kingdom of the end-time
shall last.

For the highest fulfillment of history must pass away,
like history itself, and the messianic king of the end-time
will come to an end at the end of time, along with this
time. The happiness at the end of time is only the beginning of great happiness, and as such beginning it will last
only until the end of time.[6]

In my opinion, there can be no doubt that when in the
realm of apocalyptic thought and conception there appears, alongside the new eon after the end of the old
world-era, a paradise which will pass away with this
world, two eschatological conceptions which are different in principle are being combined with each other. One
conception speaks of the divine consummation of history,
and the other anticipates salvation from the end of history.

Certainly this combination does more than serve to
accommodate already existing mythographical material.
There is a theological intention at work here also. Apparently the idea is to set forth, with the help of the
primeval-time/end-time schema, the original possibilities
of this creation, in the form of the ideal messianic interregnum. In any case, the portrayal of the paradisiacal
messianic age splendidly fulfills this function: when its

death is imminent, this world discloses and unfolds in full view how God intended it and created it for the good of mankind. In this way, in the twilight of the world there is shown the dawn of the new and better eon. In the sphere of Judaism, of course, it was necessary to ward off the gnostic danger, which lay in the two-eons schema, of denying this world to God and understanding it as evil from the outset and by its very origin. With the help of the traditional conception of the recurring paradise at the end of history, this parrying of the danger is accomplished in convincing fashion.

If at the same time the latent possibility was provided for the apocalyptist to retreat from the nonhistorical eschatology of apocalyptic to the ground of a utopian historical hope, this effect may not have been entirely unintentional; for the dehistoricizing of eschatology abandons the ground of traditional Jewish thought, while the conception of the messianic kingdom of peace represents an extreme possibility of Old Testament–Jewish eschatology.

To be sure, the essential and fundamental difference between the consummation of history in the messianic interregnum and the inbreaking of the new eon was observed and maintained. This is shown in the fact that in a number of important apocalypses a special messianic figure, the Son of Man, is introduced for the new eon which will dissolve the messianic interregnum.

The relatively few texts outside the New Testament where this figure appears all stem from the apocalyptic movement. They have been explored from all sides and with every conceivable inquiry, without a satisfactory solution of all the problems which are bound up with this enigmatic figure. We can deal with only a few questions which are of particular interest in the present context. First of all, however, the texts may be allowed to speak for themselves.

In Dan. 7, Daniel has a vision of how the eschatological judgment upon the kingdoms of this world will be fulfilled:

> . . . and behold, with the clouds of heaven came one who was like a man, and he came to the Ancient of Days, and was presented before him. And there was given to him dominion and glory and kingdom, and all peoples, nations, and tongues serve him; his power is an eternal power, which never shall pass away, and his kingdom an eternal kingdom, which is indestructible. (Dan. 7:13-14)

Further, in verse 18, we read: "and the saints of the Most High shall receive the kingdom, and they shall possess the kingdom forever." Here the "saints of the Most High" may be understood to mean the celestial angelic powers, which appear personified in the "man" of the vision.

In 4 Esdras 13:1-13 (Charles), we read:

> And it came to pass after seven days that I dreamed a dream by night: And I beheld and lo! there arose a violent wind from the sea, and stirred all its waves. And I beheld and lo! (the wind caused to come up out of the heart of the seas as it were the form of a man. And I beheld and lo!) this Man flew with the clouds of heaven. And wherever he turned his countenance to look everything seen by him trembled; and whithersoever the voice went out of his mouth, all that heard his voice melted away, as the wax melts when it feels the fire. And after this I beheld, and lo! there was gathered together from the four winds of

heaven an innumerable multitude of men to make war against the Man that came up out of the sea. And I beheld, and lo! he cut out for himself a great mountain, and flew up upon it. But I sought to see the region or place from whence the mountain had been cut out, and I could not. And after this I beheld, and lo! all who were gathered together against him to wage war with him were seized with great fear; yet they dared to fight. And lo! when he saw the assault of the multitude as they came he neither lifted up his hand, nor held spear nor any warlike weapon; but I saw only how he sent out of his mouth as it were a fiery stream, and out of his lips a flaming breath, and out of his tongue he shot forth a storm of sparks. And these were all mingled together—the fiery stream, the flaming breath, and the . . . storm; and fell upon the assault of the multitude which was prepared to fight, and burned them all up, so that suddenly nothing more was to be seen of the innumerable multitude save only dust of ashes and smell of smoke. When I saw this I was amazed. Afterwards I saw the same Man come down from the mountain, and call unto him another multitude which was peaceable. Then drew nigh unto him the faces of many men some of whom were glad, some sorrowful; while some were in bonds, some brought others who should be offered. Then through great fear I awoke.

Then follows the interpretation of this picture. The tension between picture and interpretation calls for some further remarks presently.

The "Man" frequently appears in the Similitudes of the Ethiopic Book of Enoch, where he also bears other designations such as "The Righteous One," "The Anointed One," "The Elect One," or similar messianic titles. Especially worthy of note are the following passages:

And there I saw One who had a head of days,
And His head was white like wool,
And with Him was another being whose countenance had
   the appearance of a man,
And his face was full of graciousness, like one of the holy
   angels. . . .

This is the Son of Man who hath righteousness,
With whom dwelleth righteousness,
And who revealeth all the treasures of that which is
   hidden, . . .

And this Son of Man . . .
Shall raise up the kings and the mighty from their seats,
[And the strong from their thrones]
And shall loosen the reins of the strong,
And break the teeth of the sinners . . . .[7]

And the righteous and elect shall be saved on that day,
And they shall never thenceforward see the face of the
   sinners and unrighteous.
And the Lord of Spirits will abide over them,
And with that Son of Man shall they eat
And lie down and rise up for ever and ever.
And righteous and elect shall have risen from the earth,
And ceased to be of downcast countenance.
And they shall have been clothed with garments of glory,
  . . .[8]

Two conceptions characterize the figure of the Son of
Man in a particular way: (1) He is not a man, but a
preexistent heavenly figure. (2) His primary task consists in the achievement of the judgment of the world, in
which salvation is bestowed upon the saints.

Both conceptions fit the "Son of Man" into the
apocalyptic idea of the two eons. His having been chosen
by God for his eschatological task before the creation of

the world is the assurance that *from the very beginning* God anticipated the end of this world-age and has always had in mind two eons. If God is the Lord over both eons, still he has destined the Son of Man as ruler of the new eon. The latter will destroy Azazel, the prince of this old world, and will live for ever and ever with the heavenly and earthly elect ones in a new creation without pain and guilt.

It is obvious that in this figure of the Son of Man we have to do with a special version of the messianic figure, one that is adapted to the apocalyptic scheme of eons. The judicial function is one of the constant tasks of the Messiah, even though the conception of the judgment of the world goes far beyond the old messianic ideas.

Wholly new, of course, and not prefigured in Jewish thought is the idea of preexistence, and the mythical features, such as occur particularly in 4 Esdras 13, in no way correspond to the traditional Jewish picture of the Messiah. Here one must posit alien influences, and only through the operation of such influences can the enigmatic name "Son of Man" be made comprehensible.

The figure of the Son of Man cannot be explained in terms of a development wholly within apocalyptic thought which, starting out from the traditional messianic conceptions, sketches a picture of the Messiah adapted to the two-eons idea. This is evident from the theologically unnecessary doubling of the figure of the Messiah, which shows that the Messiah–Son of Man was felt to be at least as much an innovation as a further development of an already given Jewish figure. It should be remembered that for apocalyptic thought there was no need at all to place the new eon, the rule of *God*, under the additional regency of the Son of Man. Indeed, the author of 4 Esdras apparently even regarded it as inappropriate to concede to the Son of Man the divine rule. For while the vision which came upon him in chapter 13, which tells of the preexistent "man" who rises out of the sea, sends forth a fiery stream from his mouth, and repels the assault of the evil one, obviously intends to portray the eschatological revolution of the eons, and the re-creation and reordering of the world, in his interpretation (13:25 ff.) the author is undoubtedly thinking only of the messianic interregnum and its ruler, the Messiah. In 5:56–6:6 he even wages a polemic against the view that God has a helper through whom he will bring about the change of the eons. That is to say, to the question of the seer through whom he will visit his creation, God gives the answer:

> In the beginning of the terrestrial world
>   before ever the heavenward portals were standing, . . .
> even then had I these things in mind; and through me
> alone and none other were they created; as also the End
> (shall come) through me alone and none other.
> (6:1,6 Charles)

This is an idea entirely in keeping with apocalyptic thought, which offers to the believer the unconditional assurance that ultimately in the new eon he will stand under the direct and unassailable lordship of God; even Belial, the prince of this world-age, was once a good angel of God.

Thus it is evident that the figure of the Son of Man, however much it was adapted to the apocalyptic experience of the world, can be understood only in terms of foreign influences. A generally satisfactory explanation of this mythical entity has never yet been offered. The

opinion of Bousset still seems to me to be the most
probable:

> Consequently there is the insistent surmise that in the
> figure of the *preexistent Son of Man two figures have been
> fused:* the Jewish "Messiah" and a preexistent heavenly
> being, whose source and origin is still obscure. But what
> sort this figure is, we learn from the new title: the "Son of
> Man." It is in some form the conception of the heavenly
> man (primal man), which has been combined with the
> Jewish idea of the Messiah.[9]

With all this, to be sure, the question remains open as
to what formulation of the widespread myth of the primal man lies in the background of the figure of the Son of
Man, whether and which other mythical features have
been intermingled with it, and how we are to conceive of
the process which led to the emergence of the apocalyptic Son-of-Man figure. The lack of sources makes it appear unlikely that we shall be able to do more than give a
highly hypothetical answer to this question. The only
thing evident to me is the possibility of thinking of the
mediation of a Jewish gnosis in which the primal man as
a preexistent and at the same time eschatological entity
was already blended with the Jewish figure of the Messiah. This appropriation of the figure of the Messiah,
necessary for a *Jewish* gnosis, was made possible by the
eschatological function of the gnostic *anthropos* figure;
for the gnostic "Man" not only fell into the clutches of the
demons in the primordial time, but also triumphs in the
end-time, after he has once again gathered together all
his members, victorious over the darkness. The fact that
the primal man who is scattered among all pneumatic
persons bears the name "Messiah" or "Christ" in certain

branches of Jewish gnosis shows that already early in
the gnostic movement there had occurred a blending of
the "protological" as well as eschatological figure of the
primal man with the eschatological figure of the Messiah.
We have frequently encountered interconnections between gnosis and apocalyptic, yet it cannot be determined how and where the gnostic figure of the
Messiah–primal man was transformed into the apocalyptic Son of Man.

For the understanding of apocalyptic itself, however,
the religiohistorical question as to the origin of the Son-
of-Man figure is likewise of little value. For the function
of the Son of Man in apocalyptic literature can be clearly
enough discerned. This function is that of a preexistent
Messiah who has been fitted into the two-eons scheme,
who under God's commission destroys the old eon and
reigns in the new. As this representative of the new
world-era the Son of Man stands clearly *in contrast* to
the Davidic Messiah, who does not appear in the
apocalyptic movement, and *alongside* the metamorphosis of that Messiah into the figure of the messianic
king of Paradise, who still belongs to the dying course of
this world. To this extent he is a *typically* apocalyptic
figure, and the appearance of some styles of the "Messiah," and the absence of others, are thus shown to be a
clear expression of the apocalyptic understanding of
existence and a significant criterion for the definition of
apocalyptic literature.

THE APOCALYPTIC LITERATURE

It is customary, when one describes a particular intellectual phenomenon, to begin by localizing the presentation of this phenomenon, by indicating the sources upon which the investigation is based.

We have had good reasons for taking the opposite course and waiting until almost the end of our presentation before offering some remarks about the apocalyptic literature. This literature in its proper sense does not unequivocally lend itself to identification as such; for the outward *form* of a revelational writing still is no guarantee of its apocalyptic content. And for the apocalyptists themselves, the apocalyptic content was regarded as the expression of true Judaism or Christianity; hence they could not and would not distinguish and detach a literature that was apocalyptic in *substance* from the other traditions of the faith. On the other hand, with their ideas and conceptions they also influenced the nonapocalyptic piety, so that individual ideas or even conceptual systems of apocalyptic *origin* still do not prove the substantively apocalyptic *character* of that literature in which such apocalyptic material appears.

Therefore it seemed advisable in the present case to attempt first of all, from the abundance of the traditional material that is available, to ascertain and to set forth the nature of the piety and the historical phenomenon of apocalyptic. Now, since that has been done, it is proper to look back and, on the basis of the picture that has been developed, to determine which writings are to be regarded as specifically apocalyptic, which ones only more or less fully indulge in apocalyptic thought, and which are improperly classified in the apocalyptic literature.

In the Old Testament in this connection we must mention first of all the *Book of Daniel*, which, strangely, has come down to us partly in Hebrew and partly in the Aramaic language. In genuinely apocalyptic fashion it is presented under the pseudonymous authority of Daniel, a pious man of the earlier Israelite period, and in chapters 7–12 it has him tell of his visions. These visions treat a *single* theme: the dawning, expected in the present, of the eternal kingdom of God. The author refrains from offering a justification for this expectation as such and from describing the coming kingdom in detail. He obviously is counting on his readers' actually beholding the scenes of the anticipated future. But with the help of a detailed survey of history, which Daniel is supposed to have announced during the time of the Babylonian exile, he does strive to provide proof, in chapters 2 and 7–12 of his book, that the turning point in time is now imminent.

"Now" is the reign of the Syrian king Antiochus IV ("Epiphanes"; 175–163 B.C.). The author is familiar with this king's two campaigns against Egypt (168 and 167 B.C.), as well as with the desecration of the Jewish temple which he caused at the end of the year 167. But shortly after this, "Daniel's" knowledge of the history breaks off; thus he is writing after 167, but still during the lifetime of Antiochus, perhaps at the beginning of the year 164, and he announces the great change for the present time. At the beginning of his book he presents Daniel as the exemplary Jew who had remained true to the law of the fathers even in the Babylonian imprisonment. By this means he tells who will participate in the coming kingdom of God: those Jews who remain faithful to the religion of the fathers in the present oppression by the Syrian king.

In all this, the author of the Book of Daniel, understandably, is thinking entirely in nationalistic terms: the dawning kingdom of God will bring the worldwide rule of the pious Jews. Thus apocalyptic universalism is suppressed, and one must say the same thing of apocalyptic dualism, which does not appear—at least not explicitly—in the Book of Daniel. The eternal kingdom, which is expected from God and is to destroy the earthly kingdoms and to replace them, apparently is regarded as an earthly-historical kingdom, though, to be sure, we do not learn anything more specific about it. It should not be concluded from this that Daniel represents a preliminary or early stage of apocalyptic thought. Instead, he may very well have blunted some of the points of the apocalyptic understanding of reality and thus have approximated the traditional eschatological way of thinking. It is only for this reason that his book was able to find acceptance in the Old Testament canon as a prophetic book. The contrast between the coming kingdom of God and the kingdoms of this world is also conceived of in Daniel in radically apocalyptic terms.

Along with the Book of Daniel, other apocalyptic material can, according to some, be found in the Old Testament, particularly in Isaiah 24–27. Hence it is not uncommon for the label the "Isaiah apocalypse" to be given to these chapters, which offer a separate collection of diverse eschatologically oriented pieces. But this label is not correct. It is true that the chapters contain a promise of the coming kingdom of God, and all the individual traditions of this section are summed up under the theme of the eschatological hope. But this eschatology does not show itself to be actually apocalyptic. The expectation of the resurrection of the dead, expressed in chapter 26, can no more be labeled as genuinely apocalyptic than can the hope of the kingdom of God as such. Anticipation of an imminent fulfillment is not expressed. Moreover, the literary characteristics of apocalyptic literature, particularly the portrayals of visions, are foreign to Isaiah 24–27.

Hence apocalyptic material outside the Book of Daniel cannot be identified with certainty in the Old Testament.

The *Sibylline Oracles* contain relatively early documents of apocalyptic origin. Throughout the ancient world, numerous oracular sayings were circulated under the authority of the Sibyl, a legendary seeress of remote antiquity. The Roman senate had an official collection of the utterances of the Sibyl made and consulted them in times of crisis. For its propaganda in the Roman Empire, Hellenistic Judaism took advantage of such high regard for the Sibylline Oracles by proclaiming its own message under the authority of the Sibyl. The Christians later associated themselves with this literary usage. What has remained extant and has come down to us from this entire production appears to have been collected for the first time in the sixth century, and it presents pagan, Jewish, and Christian material, with very little order and often inextricably intermingled. The Jewish sections may stem from the period from the end of the second century B.C. to the end of the second century A.D. In them the Sibyl is regarded as a daughter of Noah.

She is an unwearying preacher of monotheism and opposes all worship of idols. She underscores her propaganda for the Jewish belief in God with the prophecy of the coming judgment upon all men who worship idols. The time of judgment is portrayed in apocalyptic colors, the judgment of fire upon the world is depicted, and the destruction of Belial, the enemy of God, is described. Historical sketches, brought down to the time of the various authors, attest the Sibyl's precise foreknowledge and at the same time make it clear that the end of all things and all times is now imminent. The omens of the end are described. The Sibyl enticingly holds before the soul of the entranced pagans the wealth and the bliss of the golden kingdom of God, and in this process the Jewish national expectation recedes behind universalist motifs. All the world will come then to the splendid, newly erected temple in Jerusalem, to worship the great God who will dwell among men and will restore the era of Paradise.

The "Sibyllines" do not pursue any self-presentation of apocalyptic piety, but rather place apocalyptic motifs at the service of the comprehensive Jewish mission and propaganda. Apocalyptic conceptions which were not serviceable for such propaganda in the Hellenistic context recede into the background: the figure of the Messiah, the hope of the resurrection, and dualism;

moreover, judgment and renewal occur in the sphere of the one cosmos, outside of which there is no reality for Greek thought. Hence one cannot gather from the Sibylline Oracles a complete picture of an explicitly apocalyptic piety. Nevertheless they show how extensively the apocalyptic movement did in general influence Jewish thought in the period before and after Christ's birth.

In Genesis 5:18-24 we are told of Enoch, a descendant of Adam in the eighth generation, who because of his pious life was carried off by God. Because it was assumed on the basis of this note that Enoch lived in the celestial world close by the throne of God, many revelations were attributed to him. Three books of revelation under his name have come down to us. Best known is the *Ethiopic Book of Enoch,* so called because it has been preserved complete only in the Ethiopic translation. This purely Jewish book was greatly treasured in the Ethiopic church, while it was excised by the rest of the Christian churches and by orthodox Judaism. Its original Hebrew or Aramaic text therefore is preserved for us only in fragments, and only fragments are still extant from the Latin and the Greek translations also; the Ethiopic text is based on a Greek version.

The Ethiopic Book of Enoch consists of a series of originally independent individual writings whose ancient superscriptions are still extant in part. All the individual pieces are of more or less pronounced apocalyptic origin, and the combination of them undoubtedly was undertaken in the interest of specifically apocalyptic piety. We have quoted frequently from this work, which in modern times has attracted special attention; among the reasons for this attention is the fact that among the manuscripts and parts of manuscripts from the library of a Jewish sect that in the period around the birth of Christ had a center near the Dead Sea, which were discovered after World War II in that location, fragments of some ten manuscripts of this Ethiopic Book of Enoch or its Aramaic prototype were found. These fragments came from almost all parts of the book, with the exception of chapters 37–71, which comprise an independent book with "Similitudes," which had already frequently been regarded as a relatively late bit of tradition.

To be sure, even the Similitudes may very well come from a pre-Christian era—this question is disputed—but the individual sections of the Ethiopic Book of Enoch cannot be dated with complete certainty. The oldest pieces are usually held to be earlier than Daniel and are placed about 170 B.C.; this is true particularly of the Ten-Weeks apocalypse in chapter 93 and 91:12-17, which forms an entity in itself, while the latest sections were presumably written about a hundred years later.

In view of the fact that this Ethiopic Book of Enoch offers a collection of materials which are indeed related, but not identical in form, it is understandable that the conceptions of this book cannot all be harmonized. Thus the eschatological conceptions, for example, differ discernibly from each other. In chapters 6–36, a book marked by angelology, we find the expectation, after the great judgment, of a paradisiacal life upon the earth which has been freed from evil. The already mentioned Similitudes reach their climax in the promise of the heavenly Son of Man who will judge the sinners and then from the throne of his glory will rule over the righteous who dwell in eternal light. The "astronomical" book, chapters 72–82, gives expression at the very beginning to the expectation of a new, eternally abiding creation. The previously mentioned Ten-Weeks apocalypse also reckons on the collapse of the entire creation and the emergence of a new heaven above a world of timeless, eternal glory. In the so-called paraenetic book, chapters 91–105, the promise is given to the suffering righteous that they will be received into the heavenly world, will forever be companions of the heavenly hosts, and will be able to view, from a safe distance, the judgment upon the old eon. Regardless of what may be the source of these conceptions, they now stand together in the service of the universalistic apocalyptic hope of overcoming this world and its history.

In addition to the Ethiopic Book of Enoch, we possess a *Book of Enoch in the Slavonic language* which goes back to a Greek original and, apart from later expansions, in its core may well stem from the first century of the Christian era. To be sure, it does not contain any outlines of history or any expectation of an imminent end, but is composed predominantly of ethical admonitions which Enoch brings back to earth from his heavenly journey. Specifically apocalyptic conceptions are found only at the end of the book, in a passage of instruction about the close of earthly history and the dawning of the eternal eon. But these conceptions are presented in the context of a doctrine of "last things," which are anticipated, but in the distant future. They no longer attest any real apocalyptic understanding of existence.

Further, the *Hebrew Book of Enoch*, a writing from the second or third century A.D., is not counted in the apocalyptic literature; for in this book of rabbinical origin, Enoch tells about mysteries of the celestial world, not about the end of history.

On the other hand, the *"Assumption of Moses,"* preserved in Latin, shows itself to be heavily indebted to the apocalyptic understanding of existence. Before his death, Moses hands over to Joshua a writing with instructions about the end-time, in order that the latter may guard them as a deposit down to the last days of the world. For the author of the book, these days appear to have come in the first decades after the birth of Christ; for the survey of history which is put in Moses' mouth reaches down to this time. Thus the book was written in these decades. "From that point the times will come to an end; the course of affairs will suddenly be concluded" (7:1). Evil will be rampant. Israel in particular must suffer dreadful things under the rule of the Romans. But then God himself will appear, will give the devil his quietus, and will exalt Israel to heaven and let her behold how the earth will come to an end and will drag the heathen with it in its collapse.

The presentation of the "Assumption of Moses" exhibits "conservative" features. Universalist thought is foreign to the author, and even the idea of the resurrection is lacking. But the basic outlook of the writing nevertheless is apocalyptic: God alone acts, the material universe passes away, and a supraterrestrial kingdom will gather the righteous of Israel together.

To be sure, two other writings which we have quoted frequently, *4 Esdras* and the *Syriac Apocalypse of Baruch*, are more significant witnesses to an apocalyptic frame of mind. 4 Esdras enjoyed great popularity among the Christians of antiquity, and it has been preserved for us in many translations, while the Hebrew original has been lost. It was even included in the Latin translation of

the Bible by Jerome, the Vulgate. In the Vulgate it
follows the canonical Book of Ezra (= 1 Esdras),
Nehemiah (2 Esdras), and the apocryphal Book of Ezra
(3 Esdras, a writing whose acceptance among the Old
Testament apocrypha of his Bible Luther regarded as
not necessary), and thus appears as 4 Esdras; in the
other translations the book bears various designations.

We know no more of the author of 4 Esdras than we do
of the authors of other apocalyptic writings. But he
certainly wrote after the destruction of Jerusalem by the
Romans in the year A.D. 70 and under the impact of this
shattering experience, presumably in the last decade of
the first century. Hence he chooses as his pseudonym
the name of "Ezra," whom—significantly contrary to
historical actuality—he tries to locate in the Babylonian
exile thirty years after the destruction of Jerusalem by
Nebuchadnezzar. There Ezra received his visions, seven
in number, according to which the book was skillfully
arranged. The author has Ezra in his visions see the
heavenly world, call to God, and from an angel or from
God's own mouth receive answers to his numerous questions. The dialogues with the angel are constructed extremely dramatically. Ezra expresses the doubts and
reservations which were being uttered at the time of the
author against the apocalyptic reality of faith, while the
angel of God gives the answers which correspond to the
conviction of faith held by the apocalyptist himself.

Literarily considered, the writing is a unity, yet the
author employs numerous traditions of diverse origin,
which accounts for many of the internal tensions within
the book. Luther, who, in view of the bad experiences which he had had with the various "seers" of his
day, did not care much for such heavenly revelations,

wanted to throw the "dreamer" who had composed the Book of 4 Esdras into the Elbe River at Wittenberg. Yet this negative judgment must not be allowed to conceal the fact that the author of this book was prompted by a deep piety which in many respects is reminiscent of Paul. His writing is also an almost perfect expression of a specifically apocalyptic understanding of existence. Anyone who wishes to get to know the apocalyptic movement from the sources will do well to begin by taking up 4 Esdras.

Many students of the matter have presumed that the Syriac Apocalypse of Baruch has the same author as 4 Esdras. This surmise is based on the close connections in substance and even in wording between the two writings. Even if this thesis cannot be maintained, still it points to the close kinship of the two apocalyptic books, and therefore the basic judgment as to the genuinely apocalyptic character of the piety represented in 4 Esdras applies equally to the Syriac Book of Baruch. The author of this latter book also writes under the oppressive impact of the experience of the destruction of Jerusalem in the year 70. Hence he chooses as his pseudonymous authority Baruch, Jeremiah's scribe, who experienced the destruction of the temple in the year 587 B.C. Baruch also beholds the fall of Jerusalem, which was announced to him beforehand, and then, weeping in the ruins of Jerusalem, is informed in visions and auditory experiences about the future and about the end of the world. Like 4 Esdras, the Syriac Apocalypse of Baruch is divided into seven parts.

The book has been preserved only in the Syriac language, and that in a single manuscript which was discovered in the last century and was first made public in

1866. Only the last section, chapters 78–97, is also found in many other Syriac manuscripts, because this part, a letter of Baruch to the nine and a half tribes in the Babylonian exile, had found acceptance in the Bible of the Monophysites, a separate Syrian church. The original language of this apocalypse too may very well have been Hebrew or Aramaic, even though the Syriac translation goes back to a Greek version.

The close kinship between 4 Esdras and the Syriac Apocalypse of Baruch suggests the assumption of a dependent relationship between the two writings, but there is no unanimous opinion as to which of the two books is the earlier. If the author of 4 Esdras used the Syriac Apocalypse of Baruch, the latter would have to have been written shortly after the destruction of Jerusalem in the year 70. If it is "Baruch" that is dependent upon the other, then the first third of the second century of the Christian era comes into consideration as the time of writing of the Apocalypse of Baruch. There is less need to attempt a solution to this problem since we cannot rule out the possibility that the connections between the two books are based on the use of common traditions or on the work of a "school," so that it is not necessary to assume a direct dependence at all.

It has rightly been affirmed that the Syriac Apocalypse of Baruch is inferior to 4 Esdras in depth of religious feeling and in passion of theological thought. The reader of the two writings will agree with this judgment, though this does not imply that the Syriac Baruch is any less decidedly apocalyptic in character.

In addition to the Syriac book, there is also a *Greek Apocalypse of Baruch*, a Jewish writing from the second or third century which has undergone a Christian revision. It tells of Baruch's being caught up through five heavens, in which an angel shows him the mysteries of God. But these mysteries do not have to do with apocalyptic insights with respect to history, but with information about the destiny hereafter of both sinners and righteous ones which serves as ethical exhortation as well as with explanation concerning cosmic processes, which likewise are not set in an apocalyptic context.

All in all, hardly any explicitly apocalyptic literature can be cited other than what has already been listed. Other works that have often been cited as apocalyptic literature may indeed have the form of a revelational writing or may show themselves to have been influenced by apocalyptic conceptions, but they do not give expression to a genuinely apocalyptic understanding of existence.

Thus the lengthy *Book of Jubilees*, which probably dates from the second century B.C. and which relates, with commentary, the Old Testament story from Genesis 1 through Exodus 12, is presented as a revelation which Moses received from God on Mount Sinai. But the book does not propose to announce the imminent turning point for all things, but to spur the people of Israel of faithful observance of the Law in a pagan environment. The author is acquainted with the apocalyptic Enoch-literature (4:19), but he himself only offers apocalyptic instruction in passing, in chapter 23. This instruction contains some individual apocalyptic motifs: when sin runs rampant, the heads of the children will become white like those of old men, and an infant of three weeks will look like a hundred-year-old man; in the days of salvation which then follow, there will be no more Satan and no more evil. Yet these developments lie in the distance and are obviously regarded as events within the world and within history. The author's interest is directed to the intensifying of the Law as Israel's present and future basis of life. The threat of judgment and the promise of salvation are meant only to provide support for the ethical admonition.

The case is similar with the *"Testament of the Twelve Patriarchs,"* with which the twelve sons of Jacob are supposed, before their death, to have taken their departure from their offspring. This writing, apart from later interpolations of Christian origin which are difficult to detach from the earlier portions of the work, also dates from the second century B.C. and, besides enlargements upon biblical narratives, contains primarily moral exhortations, most of which are connected with historical examples from the Old Testament. These admonitions dwell on the background of the antagonism between God and Belial, who possesses great power over men, and not infrequently they are supported with a reference to resurrection and judgment. Like the apocalyptists, the dying sons of Jacob also foresee the fate of Israel. They know about the coming priestly king of salvation, who "will have no successor, to the most remote generations, throughout eternity." He will open the gates of Paradise and take away the sword that threatened Adam. Belial is bound, the evil spirits are trampled underfoot, and the godless cease doing evil.[1] Even the heathen who call upon God will then be saved.

However, such apocalyptic notes—the author is acquainted with the apocalyptic of Enoch—are not an expression of a basic apocalyptic understanding of existence, but auxiliary conceptions which provide emphasis for the challenge to decide now against the works of Belial, adultery and envy, murder and drunkenness, idolatry and greed, hate and exploitation, in order thus historically to make preparation for the new age.

The seventeenth Psalm of Solomon expresses a nationalist hope of the messianic king of Israel, who will destroy the opposing heathen and will rule in Jerusalem over a liberated Israel. This Israel will no longer suffer injustice, and will receive the tribute of the nations. The hope expressed here, however, is also quite far removed from the apocalyptic expectation of a new creation marked by universal peace.

Since 1947, near the Dead Sea, numerous manuscripts have been found, which belonged to a Jewish communal society who had a central point for their community in the settlement of Qumran. Among these manuscripts have been found fragments of the "Testament of the Twelve Patriarchs," the Book of Jubilees, and above all, as we have already noted, the "Ethiopic" Book of Enoch in its original Aramaic form. The members of this Dead Sea sect are regarded, with good reason, as those Essenes about whom various interesting accounts have been left us, particularly by the Jewish authors Philo and Josephus in the first century A.D. Alternatively, close connections between the two groups are indicated.

Now Adolf Hilgenfeld already held the opinion that we should see in the Essenes the connecting link between the apocalyptic circles and primitive Christianity, since "the distinctiveness of the Essenes' community system is explained only in terms of the striving of the apocalyptic school to dissociate itself from the corrupt life of the nation and to prepare for the future which was so ardently awaited."[2] Hence it is not accidental that among the most important problems for the study of the Qumran material is the question as to the relationship of the new texts to the apocalyptic view of the world. Indeed, it is not uncommon for present-day scholars to try, under the impact of the recent discoveries, to prove an "Essene" origin even for the apocalyptic movement.

One must start out from the fact that that sect which had in Qumran a kind of mother house arose when a group of pious Jews who belonged to the priestly company detached themselves from the temple in Jerusalem and the priestly aristocracy which was in control of the worship there. They did this because in their opinion the temple worship was being made unclean by the priesthood because of their inadequate observance of the legal prescriptions. Thus this point of departure for the forming of the sect betrays no apocalyptic motifs of any kind; besides, it cannot be assumed that at the time of the separation, which is usually placed in the second half of the second century B.C., apocalyptic piety played any role in the temple at Jerusalem. Moreover, no explicitly apocalyptic writings are found in the extensive body of literature that was *original* with the Dead Sea sect.[3] Of course, Daniel was known, and the Ethiopic Book of Enoch was used; but it is undoubtedly true that both writings had their origin somewhere other than in the community of Qumran.

On the other hand, the Qumran community was conscious of being the community of the end-time and counted on the imminent dawning of the time of salvation. The members of the sect were already waging the battle of the "children of light" against the "children of darkness," part of the great struggle between God and his angels on the one hand, and Belial with his demonic helpers on the other. The "War Scroll," a book especially cherished in the sect, tells in detail of the final military struggle, calculated to last forty years, of the sons of light against the children of darkness, who in the seventh and last battle are finally defeated by the sons of light. At the end God will eradicate all the unrighteous from the face of the earth, and will open to the righteous the way to eternal bliss and lasting peace without want. What is said about the "end of time," "the last generation," and "the consummation of time" may very well come from apocalyptic language. Also in harmony with apocalyptic thought is the conception of the two spirits which God has given to man "until the appointed time and the new creation. And he knows about the effects of their works at all times."

Thus Adolf Hilgenfeld may be correct insofar as the sect-situation of those pious folk of the Dead Sea caused them increasingly to be inclined toward apocalyptic conceptions. Of course, one must immediately add that eschatology was not the main concern of the pious ones of Qumran and that in the Dead Sea documents the anticipation of salvation was thought of in terms both overtly nationalistic and intrahistorical. Even the messianic conceptions are not apocalyptic, and the expectation of the resurrection of the dead is at most intimated. The final judgment and the time of salvation are never described, and one cannot fail to recognize motifs of an eschatology that pertains entirely to the present. Hence we can only speak of a certain influence of apocalyptic thought and apocalyptic concepts, as we were able to detect it also in the "Testament of the Twelve Patriarchs," which was read in the "Essene" community or even composed by it, and in the Book of Jubilees. Corresponding to this is the fact that gnosticizing influences also can be demonstrated to exist in the Qumran literature.

It would take us too far afield to sift through the whole of late Jewish literature in search of apocalyptic *motifs*. Other than those already named, documents of explicitly apocalyptic character are not found. Yet it is not uncommon for the influence of the apocalyptic thought-world, which of course was always virulent throughout Judaism, to make itself evident. This is true even when a writer like Josephus consciously avoids the "revolutionary" ideas of apocalyptic, which are hostile toward history, in order not to arouse any distrust in the Roman authorities.

We might mention further, for example, the Jewish "Life of Adam and Eve," which we have in two different versions, and which, to be sure, displays more gnostic than apocalyptic influences; the "Apocalypse of Abraham," which divides the history of the "evil eon," the dominion of Azazel, into twelve epochs; and the "Book of Elijah," a conglomeration of diverse pieces, including some of apocalyptic origin.

Even in Philo, the great Jewish theologian who wrote in Alexandria in the first century A.D., as well as in the "Book of Biblical Antiquities" which is falsely attributed to him, we find various apocalyptic passages, and of course the same holds true also of the rabbinical literature, which as a whole is anything but apocalyptically oriented, to be sure. On the contrary, Judaism threw out the apocalyptic literature earlier and more decisively than did the Christian church, and around the year 100 the famous Rabbi Akiba declared that even to take these books in one's hands was to forfeit one's salvation. Nevertheless, this did not prevent the rabbis from making use of apocalyptic ideas and conceptions from time to time, particularly in the context of eschatological pronouncements.

More productive than these last-named Jewish writings is *the early Christian literature.* We have already seen that, in spite of all the historical connections which are undoubtedly present, it is not permissible to characterize early Christianity as "apocalyptic," but that an apocalyptic native soil is clearly discernible in almost all the primitive Christian traditions. In the early Christian literature the apocalyptic texts that have been handed down stand alongside the accounts of the salvation-bringing Christ-event, in peculiar and characteristic tension. While in apocalyptic the announced *end*-events constitute the crucial occurrence, in the Christian proclamation the tradition of the salvation events that have already occurred moves into the central position. For this reason, the Jewish apocalypses that were handed down, insofar as they continued to be used in the church, were provided with references to the Christ-event.

It is still frequently disputed whether certain books with an apocalyptic flavor are of Christian origin or represent Jewish writings that have undergone Christian revision. Belonging to these traditions, which generally speaking are of little significance, are, for example, an "Apocalypse of Elijah," an "Apocalypse of Ezra" (not to be confused with 4 Esdras), and the so-called Fifth Book of Ezra, but also the interesting "Ascension of Isaiah," used particularly in the Ethiopian church.

The "Sibylline Oracles" of Christian origin refer back to apocalyptic thought-material, in order in the time of

persecution to announce to the Roman state the imminent total collapse. Borrowing from earlier apocalypses,
the Apocalypse of Thomas, only rediscovered in the
present century, tells of the omens of the end, of the
"last day," which is divided into seven days, and the
eighth day, the inbreaking of the new world. Also Christian in conception is the little apocalypse which concludes
the Didache, a little book which appeared about the year
100 or somewhat later, composed of diverse material,
most of it related to the internal order of the church.

To be sure, most of what is known by the label "early
Christian apocalypses" and is collected in the work of
Hennecke-Schneemelcher-Wilson (listed in the Bibliography) has only very little connection, or none at all,
with actual apocalyptic. This is true of the purely Christian "Apocalypse of Peter," a book widely disseminated
and often used in antiquity which probably appeared in
the first half of the second century. In contrast to the
canonical "Apocalypse of John," for example, this book
shows no interest in the end of history, but is interested
in the hereafter, whose celestial joys and hellish torments are depicted in order to underscore the admonition to repentance. The same may be said, for example,
of the "Apocalypse of Paul," which tells of what Paul is
supposed to have experienced during the time when he
was caught up into Paradise, mentioned in 2 Cor. 12:1 ff.
The same is true also of the "Shepherd of Hermas," a
"prophetic" book from the end of the second century
which for a long time enjoyed canonical recognition in
the church in many areas. In the fourth Vision it appro-
priates some interesting apocalyptic material; however, the author of the "Shepherd" does not interpret and
use this traditional material in the sense of an apoc-

alyptic eschatology and perspective on existence.

On the whole, therefore, one finds most of the apocalyptic material that appears within the Christian tradition in the New Testament itself, primarily of course in the Apocalypse of John and in the synoptic apocalypse in Mark 13 and parallels, both of which make heavy use of Jewish traditions. But in 2 Thess. 2:1-12 also there appears an interesting apocalyptic passage of apparently Jewish origin, while in 1 Thess. 4:16 Paul in his own words portrays the future Parousia of the heavenly Christ in an apocalyptic manner. The Second Epistle of Peter defends against scoffers the primitive Christian expectation of the Parousia in view of the evident delay of the end-events, and in so doing works with apocalyptic materials, particularly in chapter 3. If one adds to all this the apocalyptic terminology already used by Paul, with the help of which the situation of the Christian in the world is described as eschatological existence, one can easily extract from the New Testament a complete outline of history and on this basis unfold in all its dimensions, and document, the essence of apocalyptic piety. Thereby we gain an admittedly indirect but relatively early and readily datable witness for a fully developed apocalyptic.

It is understandable that no outlines of history have been incorporated into the New Testament literature by the help of which the present would be shown to be the last time; people were already looking back to the decisive turning point toward which all history pointed. Instead, in general, warnings are given against calculations of the end. "No one knows about that day and that hour, neither the angels in heaven, nor the Son, but only the Father" (Matt. 24:36). Nevertheless the primitive community lives in the reminiscence of apocalyptic expectation of the imminent end: "This generation will not pass away before all this happens" (Mark 13:30). "If I by the Spirit of God drive out of the demons," says Jesus (Matt. 12:28), "then the kingdom of God has indeed come very near to you." Hence the admonition to constant watchfulness remains the crucial point (Mark 13:33-37); one may observe the "signs of the times," for they are the omens of the end (Mark 13:28-29; Matt. 16:3). The time still remaining for this world is short; one should be ready. This world is about to pass away (1 Cor. 7:29-31); its end is near (Rev. 1:1-3; 1 Cor. 10:11). Jesus saw Satan fall like lightning from heaven (Luke 10:18).

For "this" eon, "this" world (Eph. 2:2), along with the demonic forces which govern it, is perishable (1 Cor. 2:6, 8). Heaven *and* earth must pass away (Mark 13:31). The fall of the first man has brought corruption into "this" world (Rom. 5:12), and the whole creation was drawn into this corruption (Rom. 8:19 ff.). Thus the devil became the "god of this eon" (2 Cor. 4:4);[4] the entire present eon must be characterized as "evil" (Gal. 1:4), and the wisdom of "this" world is folly (1 Cor. 3:18). To be sure, there are, among this "crooked and perverse generation," the host of the righteous, the blameless "children of God," who shine in this eon like stars in the heavens (Phil. 2:15).

But now the time granted to this eon has run its course (Mark 1: 15); it is "full" (Gal. 4:4). The death struggle of the old eon begins. Satan is still being held in check, but soon the "lawless one" will begin to rage (2 Thess. 2:3 ff.; Rev. 12). "Then let the inhabitants of Judea flee to the mountains. Anyone who is on the housetop should not go down and enter the house to take anything away. Anyone who is in the field should not run back to get his cloak. . . . In those days there will be more distress than ever since the beginning of the world which God created, up until today" (Mark 13:14 ff.). If God did not shorten the last days, even his righteous ones who are chosen for the new eon could not survive (Mark 13:20).

The coming of the Son of Man brings the turning point: the judgment upon this eon and for the righteous ones of the new eon (Mark 13:26-27). Corruption will suddenly come upon the old eon (1 Thess. 5:1ff.). As a bolt of lightning lights up the whole earth all at once, so will the Son of Man appear at the same time everywhere (Matt. 24:27). He will destroy Satan with the breath of his mouth (2 Thess. 2:8). The dead will rise and along with the living righteous ones will be caught up to the Lord, to be united forever with him (1 Thess. 4:16; Phil. 3:20; 1 Cor. 15:52). The "Revelation of John" knows of the thousand-year interregnum between the old and the new course of the world (Rev. 20:1 ff.), which will be followed by the final destruction of Satan. Then heaven and earth will pass away (Mark 13:31; Rev. 21:1).

In the new eon *everything* is new (Rev. 21:5). It cannot be described, but it brings "what no eye has seen and no ear has heard, and what has never entered into the heart of man" (1 Cor. 2:9), a *new* creation and a *new* man (Rev. 21:2; 2 Cor. 5:17; Rom. 12:2). Flesh and blood, on the other hand, cannot inherit the kingdom of God (1 Cor. 15:50). Time is no more (Rev. 10:6). Men are like the angels in heaven (Mark 12:18 ff.). Even the sun and the moon no longer shine, and day and night disappear; for God is the light of men (Rev. 21:23 ff.). The servants become sons (Gal. 4:7; Rev. 21:7). Love, peace, and joy will reign in the kingdom of God (Gal. 5:21-22). Men will live in undisturbed communion with God (1 Thess. 4:17; Rev. 21:3) for ever and ever (Rev. 22:1ff.).

In our presentation of apocalyptic piety we have deliberately refrained from referring to these and other items of documentation from the New Testament, because, as a rule, in their Christian context they are no longer a direct expression of an apocalyptic understanding of existence. As we have just seen, they can be lifted out of their context and fitted together into a comprehensive picture of apocalyptic thought and belief. This can serve to confirm the correctness of the outline of genuine apocalyptic piety developed in this book, and at the same time it documents the fact that dualistically stamped apocalyptic must have been formed in Judaism by the beginning of the Christian era at the latest.

In this connection the following observations are also interesting. At the center of the apocalyptically oriented preaching of Jesus stands the concept of the "kingdom of God." Jesus evidently uses this concept only in the futuristic sense, and with it he denotes the coming eon in which the dominion of evil will be broken and God alone will rule. This concept is indeed already used in the Book of Daniel in this way,[5] but otherwise it plays no role in the apocalyptic literature, even though it emerges in isolated instances. Correspondingly, the sharply dualistic designation of Satan as the god or the prince of this world does indeed appear in the New Testament,[6] but not in original apocalyptic literature, even though, like the concept of the kingdom of God, which is central in Jesus' preaching, he must stem from the apocalyptic tradition.

Such examples show that the literary documents which testify to the apocalyptic movement are able to cover only a slight portion of what thrived in this movement itself in the course of time. Hence it is a difficult and not very promising undertaking, on the basis of the accidentally preserved and often hardly datable apocalyptic literature, to sketch out with any measure of certainty a *development* in apocalyptic piety and its thought-world.

Therefore in this chapter, as elsewhere, we have refrained from undertaking the certainly legitimate task of distinguishing the various stages or local forms of apocalyptic. Even a successful fulfillment of this task, of course, may very well prove in essence to underscore the *unitary* character of apocalyptic piety rather than to call it in question.

THE HISTORICAL EFFECTS
OF APOCALYPTIC

Apart from the Book of Daniel and the Revelation of John, the apocalyptic literature did not gain entrance into the official canon of the synagogue and the Christian church. An exception is provided only by 4 Esdras, which was lost in the Hebrew and Greek forms—thus the synagogue as well as the church of the East rejected the book—but remained extant in the Vulgate, the Latin translation of the Bible by Jerome.

Yet the amount of apocalyptic literature that continued to be preserved was not negligible; this was true above all because of the interest in this literature in individual, mostly remote, areas of the Christian church. This explains, on the one hand, the fact that the extant Jewish apocalypses not infrequently display more or less extensive evidences of Christian revision, and, on the other hand, the peculiar state of affairs whereby most of the pieces of this literature have come down to us, not in the original Hebrew, Aramaic, or Greek language, but only in Ethiopic, Syriac, Slavic, Armenian, Coptic, Latin, and other translations.

The Apocalyptic Movement

In those Christian circles which cultivated an interest in apocalyptic, there was also the new production of more or less specifically apocalyptic writings, in which it was not uncommon for Jewish materials to be appropriated. The "Revelation of John" is the best-known of these Christian apocalypses and the only one to gain admission into the New Testament canon. The rest of the writings which belong to this group are for the most part of little value; we have already mentioned the most important of them.[1]

Now and then scholars are disposed, upon reading this last-named body of literature, to speak of a re-apocalypticizing of the primitive Christian message. But one must not overlook the fact that the Christian apocalypses were not very influential, and they owe their emergence, as a rule, to particular historical situations. Particularly in times of persecution there arose a strong yearning for an early end to this world. Then, as was already the case in the Apocalypse of John, the hope of redemption from this eon was combined particularly with the prediction of judgment upon Rome:

There will fall upon you, haughty Rome, the sudden
Lightning bolt from on high, and you will first bow your
  neck;
You will be leveled to the ground, and the fire will wholly
  consume you,
Cowering on your own soil; your wealth will pass away,
And then wolves and foxes will inhabit your lands.
And then you will be utterly abandoned, as though you
  did not exist.
Where then is your palladium? And which god will save
  you?
One of gold or iron or silver? Where then will be

Your senate's decrees? Where Rhea's and Kronos'
genealogy?
Or your descent from Zeus and all that you revere?[2]

In Christian apocalypses from such difficult times the
end-events and the new eon itself are of less interest
than the promising portents of the end which are presently discernible, and an explicitly apocalyptic understanding of existence can hardly be detected, even
though there certainly is a hope of a great change to be
wrought by God. The judgment upon Rome is evidently
anticipated as an event within history.

This development is as characteristic as it is understandable. Wherever theology is practiced in the sphere
of influence of the Christian proclamation, apocalyptic
thought and belief in the genuine sense cannot prevail.
The basic Christian doctrine of God's becoming man, the
incarnation of the Logos, the redemption of the cosmos,
the dawning within history of the new eon, makes any
dualism that totally rejects the world and history a
heresy. Therefore the Christian churches have always
set themselves just as consistently against any apocalyptic fanaticism as against gnostic enthusiasm. Apocalyptic
and enthusiasm are the outwardly very different but
inwardly closely related siblings which were never
acknowledged by the church as legitimate children, even
where they grew up in her bosom.

In the Christian West, therefore, apocalyptic could
appear only as a peripheral phenomenon, and the positive influence of apocalyptic literature could be achieved
only as an appropriation of apocalyptic conceptions and
motifs into an essentially nonapocalyptic way of thinking, as we have already observed in the New Testament

itself. It is only in post-Christian movements that apocalyptic itself has been able again to achieve significant success.

In the literature of the early church the authors like to paint the terrors of the end and of hell, using the devices of apocalyptic, in order to spur the reader to the continuing struggle against evil and to challenge him to constant watchfulness against all the deceitful attacks of the devil. Thus the apocalyptic tradition entered into the service of ethical admonition. In this process, the problem of time, which was constitutive for apocalyptic, was bracketed out.

Accordingly, the "revelations" of the various seers hardly ever have as their goal the events of the end, but rather the world of the blessed and the damned hereafter, into which man will enter after his death. In the "Apocalypse of Peter" and the "Apocalypse of Paul," the places of punishment of the sinners and the torments of hell are portrayed in detail to the two apostles, the latter on an extended journey through heaven, but the joys of the blessed in Paradise are also appealingly set before their eyes. Therewith the territory of apocalyptic thought is completely left behind.

This corresponds to the development of the early Catholic church on the whole, which is more and more open to Greek thought and transposes the eschatological expectations out of the temporal pattern of "now-then" into the spatial pattern of "below-above." The present becomes the time of individual preparation for the salvation which lies waiting for us, timelessly, in the world above. The hope of the future is not so much oriented to the end of the world as to the salvation of souls after death. The doctrine of purgatory in which the individual soul is purified displaces the expectation of the cosmic firestorm at the end of time. The final judgment becomes less significant, giving way to the individual judgment after death and the system of penance and absolution connected with it. The sacraments guarantee a salvation that is not of the future, but in the heavenly realm.

It is true that occasionally the rejection of history which is a familiar theme in apocalyptic breaks through. This happens, at least in incipient fashion, among the Alexandrians in the third century and in monastic groups and mystical circles. Generally speaking, however, this does not happen on the basis of a temporal eschatological expectation of the end of the world, but on the basis of a being-oriented, gnosticizing dualism of world and heaven, history and spirit: the human spirits are purified by degrees and are led back to the deity which is their source, until at last all are saved and the old course of the world, the material world, comes to an end.

At the same time, interest in the end of time and of the world in general is flagging. The church as the legally structured institution of salvation bridges the period from Jesus' first coming to the end of history at his return. Tyconius and Augustine equate the thousand-year kingdom which is to precede the end with the age of the church. They are able in this way to historicize in a thoroughgoing fashion an important apocalyptic conception. Thereby at the same time they push the end of the world into the remote distance, even if the number one thousand was not understood literally. In general, the church has regarded with mistrust and has restricted an intensified interest in a temporally conceived eschatology and the negative and revolutionary feeling of apocalyptic which is easily related to that eschatology.

Nevertheless, the apocalyptic passages in the New Testament are preserved, and in spite of the many voices raised in opposition, particularly in the eastern part of the empire, the Revelation of John finally gained acceptance into the canon of the New Testament in the fourth century. Thereby apocalyptic eschatology's ideas about the goal of history remained an important element in the Christian tradition and a part of dogmatics. Apocalyptic maintained its possibilities of exerting influence, and it could make itself manifest from time to time.

Viewed as a whole, the greatest significance of apocalyptic in this regard consists in the fact that it played an important part in mediating to the West the teleological way of thinking about history, that is, the idea of a definitive goal and end of history. This idea makes it possible, in principle, to survey and interpret history as a whole, and to understand any given point in terms of the historically overarching reality. This way of comprehending reality, which apparently was imparted to Jewish apocalyptic from Iran, was foreign to the Old Testament, as it was to the Greeks; for in the Greek view, history runs its course in cycles, after the analogy of nature: after the expiration of a world-year it returns once again to its beginning. The Old Testament, on the other hand, does indeed know a linear way of thinking about history, but it does not conceive of history in terms of a goal, in the sense that sooner or later it will come to a definitive end. Apocalyptic introduced this idea into the Western tradition, even though the way was prepared for it by postexilic Judaism.

To be sure, it did not become fruitful in the West, in general, in the apocalyptic sense, but in a form adapted to biblical thought. For in apocalyptic there is no positive interest in history combined with the insight into the completed course of history. One could and had to speak of the unity of history, because one believed himself to be standing at the end of the course of history and awaited the new eon which now would bring all history to its well-deserved end. Indeed, even the surveys of past history which are found in apocalyptic do not exhibit a positive attitude toward history, but only the strong hope for the end of history.

In the Western tradition, on the other hand, the possibility of viewing history as a whole often intensifies the interest in history itself and leads to the attempt to infer in general what is actual from the totality of the historical phenomenon and to give to the world-event a meaning in terms of its historical goal. The philosophy of history is rooted in this soil, as a genuinely Western phenomenon, one which was significantly stimulated by the original apocalyptic conception of history. The question as to the meaning of history could after all arise only in such a context. In this connection, in the Middle Ages the picture of history minted by Augustine in *The City of God* was predominant, a view which regarded history since the fall of man as a way toward consummation of the kingdom of God. Christ is the turning point in this history. With him there begins the thousand-year kingdom of the final struggle with the satanic powers, a struggle in which Christians are actively involved and in which the final victory will belong to Christ's side.

When, at the beginning of modern times, the authority of the biblical revelation to which this picture of history appealed disappeared, there appeared in place of the outline of history drawn from the Bible an interpretation of history gained from empirical history. Thus out of the old question as to the meaning of history there now arose the search for the historical reality itself with which people wished to answer that question. There began the age of historicism, in which we still stand and whose own history therefore cannot yet be definitively described.

But regardless of how historical interest has been manifested in the past two hundred years, in the last analysis it is defined by the search for the meaning of history as a whole, and therefore it cannot be comprehended apart from crucial but decisively modified influences of the apocalyptic construction of history. Even positivistic historicism, which denies any meaning of history as a whole, still stands, with this denial, within the inquiry about the meaning of the whole of history which was mediated primarily through apocalyptic. The same is true of the undertaking, so necessary for the modern world and presently in process of development, of planning for the future with the help of scientific projections (futurology), whenever it is bound up with ideological-utopian designs for the future.

In this connection, in the course of history changing attitudes toward the basic apocalyptic schema are exhibited in matters of detail. Not infrequently there is a direct renewal of the original apocalyptic situation, in that people believe themselves to be standing at the end of history and expect in their own time the dawning of the kingdom of God, whose coming has been so long delayed. To be sure, in keeping with the Christian ties with history, the expectation is primarily oriented not to a new eon which negates history and the old creation as such, but to a final kingdom in history. The expectations of the end are concentrated on the *inter*regnum of the apocalyptic outline of history, and it is only with difficulty that we can determine when, in the utopian pictures of the kingdom of God at the end of history, the heretical apocalyptic decision against history itself is making itself heard.

The sense of the present as the end-time appears again in the Montanism of the second century, with an intense expectation of the imminent end, but already at this time it is critically regarded by the Great Church. Around the year 1000 many expect the expiration of the thousand-year kingdom and the end of the world; this contributes temporarily to an increased interest in the final judgment (Peter Lombard).

Joachim of Floris (died 1202) calculates the periods of history again in connection with the dogma of the Trinity and expects the age of the Father and that of the Son to be followed in 1260 with the dawn of the age of the Holy Spirit as the final epoch which will bring full salvation— to be sure a speculative historicizing of apocalyptic eschatology, which, however, repeatedly stimulated the rise of apocalyptic expectations of the end, particularly among the Franciscan Spirituals.

Joachim himself tells, not incidentally, that his vision of history came to him while he was reading the Apocalypse of John. In calculating in advance the future events on the basis of the earlier course of history, he becomes a prophet in the style of the apocalyptic interpreter of history. In the coming kingdom of the Spirit the Sermon on the Mount is to become the basis of the ordering of society, perfect love is to take the place of law, and men will have transcended human status to arrive at an angel-like status, so that the new society may thus be actualized. In these expectations we encounter thoroughly apocalyptic conceptions of goals, though, to be sure, in historical form; and it is not accidental that Joachim represents a strong asceticism which is supposed to guard against all contacts with this world as far as possible.

The earliest biography of Joachim, written in 1228 by Thomas of Celano, "begins with a kind of critique of culture. . . . The children grow up in the prejudices of their parents and, out of fear of 'harsh punishment' by this power, which has become the *lex publica*, no one dares to resist. So from the very outset, the inclination toward the good in the children is stifled by the parents, who are guilty of everything. . . . Here the metaphysical view of original sin . . . has been transformed into a kind of sociological doctrine of original sin, which sees in original sin the social convention and the public opinion into which the uncorrupted person is born."[3] This is entirely in keeping with the apocalyptic understanding of existence, for which this world is so hopelessly corrupt that one can only hope for a new world.

While Joachim still places himself entirely within the second world-era, the provisional time of the Son, the Spirituals, who appeal to Joachim and revere St. Francis as a new redeemer and bearer of the Spirit, claim already to be living in the new age. Not infrequently, they draw revolutionary conclusions from this understanding of time, in view of the ongoing old world. They wish to do all they can to bring about the new. Hence they turn not only against the papal church, but, above all, against the imperial policies of the Hohenstaufen. The emperor, especially Frederick II, who regarded himself as the eschatological king of peace, was held to be the Anti-

christ, just as already in ancient apocalyptic the Roman
state appears as the beast from the abyss. When Frederick II died in 1250 without being destroyed, in accordance with their predictions, by the inbreaking of the
new eon, and when the world-judgment which had been
announced by Joachim did not occur, the Spirituals fell
into a grave crisis.

The apocalyptic-gnostic idea of bringing *new* revelations is quite familiar to the Spirituals, and it is likewise
in keeping with apocalyptic thought when these revelations are constantly concerned with the interpretation of
the present closing history of the old eon. Sects are
formed, in which the perfect ones come together, the
bearers of the Spirit, who know the *kairos,* and who in
radical renunciation of possessions and marriage demonstrate their rejection of this disintegrating eon, in
order to be able, in the now inbreaking new eon, after
the destruction of the "massa perditionis," to rule as the
band of righteous ones. Chiliastic utopian societies are
often combined with the expectation of the coming eon;
this is in harmony with the apocalyptic juxtaposition of
the messianic kingdom at the end of history and the
coming kingdom of God.

In the pre-Reformation period, particularly among
those theologians who were suffering severely under the
unsatisfactory conditions in the church, there arose
apocalyptic speculations, which, to be sure, were still
more heavily dominant in wide circles among the laity
who felt a special appeal in the attacks made by the
Franciscans in opposition to the wealth of the church. In
the socially oppressed strata in the fourteenth and fif-
teenth centuries there was a quite general expectation of
the revolution of the times and the dawning of the golden

age. Beguines and Beghards, constantly under suspicion of heresy, carried more or less apocalyptic ideas among the people, until, in consequence of the Reformation and the turning back to biblical Christianity, this kind of eschatology was pushed into a corner.

Apocalyptic ideals such as the elimination of private property and the eradication of mortal sins were actualized by the Taborites, the radical group among the adherents of John Huss, after his death (1415). They expected that in 1420 the Taborite company would be gathered home by the coming Christ. Then "there will be no king or ruler or subject on earth, and all taxes and tributes will cease; no one will compel another to do anything, for all will be equal brothers and sisters. There will be neither masters nor slaves, neither sinners nor sufferers."

Pre-reformers and reformers see in the pope the Antichrist, who appears before the end; thus even Luther can occasionally announce the end of the world as imminent, just as many reformers in general like to call their time the last time, the evening of the world. With Zwingli, to be sure, under humanistic influence apocalyptic thinking entirely recedes, and eschatological fanatics, who in many places are connected with spiritualist circles and the baptist movement and at times seek to bring in the kingdom of God with armed force, soon discredit for all reformers the radical speculations about the end-time. The Reformation catechisms contain no eschatological statements of an apocalyptic sort; Article VII of the Augsburg Confession rejects the chiliasm of the fanatics as Jewish doctrine. Luther sharply dissociates himself from the socially revolutionary ideas of Thomas Münzer, who died in the Peasants' War in 1525, from the inspired prophet of the end-time Melchior Hofmann, and from the communistic fanaticism of Bernd Rothmann and his friends in Münster, whose activity altogether points to the latent influence of the socially revolutionary ideas in the closing years of the Middle Ages, ideas which were closely akin to apocalyptic thought.

Yet apocalyptic eschatological expectations continue to have a vitality and are intensified in times of epidemic, in the Thirty Years' War, and wherever, since the time of the Counter-Reformation, minorities have lived under persecution and oppression and have hoped for deliverance from their plight.

Particularly within Pietist circles, then, all sorts of speculations about the inbreaking of the millennium reappear. Following the example of Jacob Boehme, for example, Philipp J. Spener connects the exposition of Rev. 20 with the optimistic expectation of a better time for the church in the future, and the Swabian Pietist Oetinger involves the entire universe in the hope of salvation-history; for, he says, "materiality is the end of God's paths."

Many of the present-day sects have their origin in eschatological expectations which predict the end of the world in the near future. The group of the Adventists, for example, is formed on the basis of the calculation by W. Miller that Christ would come again in 1843/44 to establish the millennium. At the origin of the Catholic Apostolic Church, as well as of the New Apostolic Church, there stood the conviction that in preparation for the return of Christ twelve apostles had to stand ready; in 1835 these actually came together and in company awaited the events of the end. The movement of the Jehovah's Witnesses is grounded in the assertion of

C. T. Russell that Christ had returned in secret in 1874, and in 1914 would begin his reign in the thousand-year kingdom. The Jehovah's Witnesses' rejection in principle of the power of the state clearly indicates the apocalyptic-anarchistic tendency of this influential sect, which some, with good reason, have regarded as a Jewish rather than a Christian group.

The striking increase in apocalyptic fanaticism since the eighteenth century is related to the general breakthrough of the historical consciousness which came at that time, a consciousness which also led to numerous conceptions of an eschatologically oriented theology of salvation history. This is represented in the eighteenth century, for example, by Johann A. Bengel, who calculated the date of the end of the world as the year 3836, and by Johann J. Hess, who composed the first "Life of Jesus"—a clear sign of historical interest—and in 1774 wrote a salvation-historical treatment of dogmatics under the title *Von dem Reiche Gottes. Ein Versuch über den Plan der göttlichen Anstalten und Offenbarungen* [On the kingdom of God. An essay on the plan of the divine agencies and revelations]. In the nineteenth century it is represented, among others, by J. C. K. von Hofmann, who on the basis of the Bible arranged the whole of history into a schema of prophecy and fulfillment. The prime example in modern times is Oscar Cullmann, who understands Christ to be the "center of time," which is moving toward its end along an irregular line. These salvation-historical outlines of theology hold, in principle, to the Christian-Augustinian outline of history. They exhibit their closeness to apocalyptic thought above all in the fact that they view history as a unitary reality which is moving toward a definitive goal; yet, in contrast to the apocalyptic experience of existence, they understand the goal of history as the fulfillment of history as well. Hence they are often interested in the time of history, not primarily in the end-time.

Wolfhart Pannenberg and Jürgen Moltmann are among the influential contemporary theologians whose outlines are heavily influenced by apocalyptic eschatology. Pannenberg regards the resurrection of Jesus as a prolepsis of the end-event. Anyone who takes his position at the resurrection of Jesus is therefore able already in advance to survey the course of history from the perspective of its end and consequently, by including that portion of history that remains yet to be accomplished, to understand it as having meaning. Pannenberg's claim to be able to evaluate history as a whole betrays the apocalyptic origin of his conception, and hence it is not accidental that he appeals primarily to Jewish apocalyptic and to the apocalyptic passages in the New Testament. To be sure, in such an appeal he and his friends overlook the fact that the outlines of history appearing in the apocalyptic literature exhibit no positive interest in history but stand in the service of a denial of history. Furthermore, they misunderstand the New Testament as well when they interpret the Christ-event as a prolepsis of the end, while in primitive Christianity the coming of Christ was (dialectically) proclaimed as the end of the old world-age itself.

Moltmann sketches a theology of hope from the perspective of the resurrection of Jesus, a theology which teaches us to concentrate all our energies on the apocalyptic final goal of history, or on the final kingdom which will be the consummation of history; for the resurrection of Jesus announces the end of the world as the end of misery, injustice, and perishability. "The social revolution of overturning unjust conditions is the immanent obverse side of the transcendental hope of the resurrection."

In all the theological currents just described, history appears in the context of a dualistic conception as a battleground between good and evil, and the ultimate victory of good occurs "providentia et auctoritate Dei" ("by the providence and authority of God"), in which a final and decisive intervention by God remains constantly in view.

Alongside this outlook, there has always been found the idealistic view that the good powers of man will develop more and more toward perfection, until at last in this way the kingdom of humanity emerges as the goal of God's ways. The trailblazers for this kind of thinking, in which the Greek pictures of man and the world are combined with the apocalyptic teleology, were the Humanists, particularly Erasmus of Rotterdam, who wanted to see the kingdom of God as a universal kingdom of peace already realized in earthly society. Without any question, this humanist conception, with its denial of the power of evil and its optimism about progress within history, exhibits an essentially nonapocalyptic understanding of reality. But just as idealism often allied itself with gnosticizing tendencies by seeing the perfected spirit of the individual being merged with the divine spirit, so also in idealist thought it is not uncommon to encounter the apocalyptic conception of history being perfected.

For Fichte, one of the major representatives of German idealism, man here on earth can achieve the rest, peace, and blessedness of the kingdom of God wherever and whenever he will, in that he understands himself, in his spirit, as part of the Absolute and rests and stands firm in the *One*. Yet Fichte does combine this pure idealism with eschatological motifs: the more men realize within themselves the kingdom of God as a moral, spiritual kingdom, the more it will prevail in the external world as well. Man must be schooled according to reason "until the race exists in reason as a perfected imprint of its eternal prototype, and thus the goal of earthly life is reached, the end of that earthly life appears, and humanity treads the loftier spheres of eternity." ". . . At last all must enter into the safe harbor of eternal rest and blessedness; at last the kingdom of God must appear, and his might and power and glory."

Fichte is followed by Schelling, who however also refers back to Joachim of Floris when he adduces the most important apostolic figures of the New Testament for the interpretation of history in such a way that Peter, the apostle of the Father, represents Catholicism, Paul, the apostle of the Son, the age of Protestantism, and John, the apostle of the Spirit, the religion of perfected humanity.

It was Hegel who above all combined the idealistic and the historical approach. The spirit does not stand over against historical reality as a general idea, but is realized *in* the particular; everything real is spiritual, and everything spiritual is real. In the self-awareness of the thinking spirit the being-for-self of the universal spirit here on the one hand, and of the particular spirit, which historically and naturally arises out of it, on the other hand, is taken up in an ideal unity. "The goal, which is Absolute

Knowledge or Spirit knowing itself as Spirit, finds its pathway in the recollection of spiritual forms [*Geister*] as they are in themselves and as they accomplish the organization of their spiritual kingdom," as it is put in the closing words of *The Phenomenology of Mind* (G. W. F. Hegel, *The Phenomenology of Mind*, trans. J. B. Baillie, 2d ed. [New York: The Macmillan Co., 1931], p. 808). Thus this self-unfolding of the spirit develops along historical lines, and indeed, as is the case in apocalyptic, according to unalterable laws; only it is not God who prescribes for history her laws from without, but the divine spirit that is immanent in history, that prescribes them from within history. In place of the divine providence which from the very beginning created two eons, there appears the "cunning of the [spiritual] reason," which also makes unconscious human activity and the apparently meaningless and destructive in history serviceable to the intention of the spirit. The end of history is reached when the spirit in thinking awareness comes to itself, when it acquires in man absolute knowledge about itself; thus it is practically achieved in the Christian philosophy of religion of Hegel himself, on the basis of which church and state also will come together in a rational social order. "May the kingdom come, and may our hands not be idle," wrote Hegel to Schelling in 1795. This kingdom of the divine spirit is actualized in history, and the eschatological judgment of the world coincides with the history of the world as a whole.

The representatives of the Enlightenment and the Romanticists also offer an illumination of the reality of history, no less intensively than the Idealists, though in a different way. Turgot (died 1781) is the earliest influential representative of an enlightened speculation about history. He believed in a divine providence over the whole course of history, in which, to be sure, men themselves have an ever-increasing share of the activity, so that he conceives of history as the march of an immense army which is directed by a powerful genius. After the theological and the metaphysical age, the rational age dawns, in which people are scientifically oriented and informed about progress. With Turgot's pupil Condorcet (died 1794), the belief in the progress of civilization was heightened into the idea of the imminent perfection of a world without conflicts, tyrants, and criminals, filled with peace, freedom, and reason; and Condorcet did not doubt that this development could be counted on, almost as surely as a law of nature.

There was not far to go from such ideas of the Enlightenment to early socialism. From a more or less revolutionary assimilation of the circumstances of production to the expanding powers of production, anyone who had a clear eye for the beginning technical revolution could easily anticipate the dawning of the splendid new era. Thus this way from the Enlightenment to socialism was at the same time the way from the more predominantly Greek and cosmic ideas of the utopias of the ideal world to the more stoutly apocalyptic hope of the perfect goal of the course of history.

William Godwin (1756–1836), for example, originally a theologian, hoped for earthly immortality for man when the spirit has at last achieved rule over matter, because then property will be justly apportioned, the state will have vanished, crime will have ceased, and individual compulsions will have come to an end. "The men therefore whom we are supposing to exist, when the earth shall refuse itself to a more extended population, will probably cease to propagate. They will no longer have any motive, either of error or reason, to induce them. The whole will be a people of men, and not of children." [4] Saint-Simon (1760–1825) announced that through economic planning an earthly paradise could be achieved which would bring an end to this wretched age and would even surpass the Paradise of the beginning. Wilhelm Weitling expects the communist community of property to result in humanity "as it should be," a world filled with carefree people who never lose hope and patience; there is an abundance of everything the heart desires; every day is Sunday; work will no longer be a burden; all wishes that are not intemperate and excessive will be fulfilled.

In the eighteenth century there flourished a type of novel which, in the various individual works, provides a utopian portrayal of the perfect world, whether this is thought of as incapable of realization or as a realistic utopian goal. Numerous thinkers reflect upon the changes necessary to produce a new world, in which the new in some cases represents a return to the uncorrupted ancient world, and in other cases an advance to an unknown new world. For example, in the middle of the eighteenth century Dom Deschamps describes, in a radically secularized and discernibly apocalyptic fashion, the future world as the definitive state of salvation which will not exhibit historical change and will be devoid of unresolved conflicts. It is a world without property, without law and punishment, without marriage and family relationships. Luxury will be abolished; there will no longer be any distinction between ordinary days and holidays, or between rest and labor. In this world the children will educate themselves. All needs will be gratified. Men will so nearly approximate the same relationships to each other that fewer differences will exist among them than among animals of the same species. Thus jealousy and rivalry will vanish. It is the world which no eye has yet seen and no ear has heard, and Dom Deschamps thinks that he cannot adequately describe this world, because it differs, in every respect and in the highest measure, from any historical reality that can be experienced.

Most of the German representatives of the Enlightenment think in more sober terms and, at the same time, more historically. They stand in closer connection with biblical historical thinking than do the French utopians and representatives of the Enlightenment; the latter more closely follow the pattern of the utopias of a perfectly ordered cosmos, and thus are heirs of the Greek spirit. Lessing, in his essay "Die Erziehung des Menschengeschlechts" [The education of the human race], portrays history as an educational process issuing from God, whereby the mature man is produced, who will do only the good, and this only for the sake of the good. ". . . It will come, it will surely come, this time of fulfillment. . . . It will surely come, the time of a new and eternal gospel, which is promised to us in the very fundamental books of the New Covenant." Herewith Lessing is explicitly referring to Joachim of Floris' teaching about the ages of the world; the only thing he found in that teaching worthy of reproof was the belief that the "third kingdom" would come suddenly, whereas in his view eternal providence is turning the wheel of history toward perfection only imperceptibly.

For Herder, too, all God's ways in history point toward the divine kingdom of a perfect *humanitas*. Kant anticipates the kingdom of God as worldwide ethical community, indeed as the end of a "progressive movement towards infinity" of humanity itself, which is involved in "continuous advance and approach toward the loftiest good that is possible on earth." In labeling this view "chiliasm," Kant rightly observes not only the close connection of the religious eschatology of the Pietists with the secularized eschatology of the Enlightenment of that time, but also the rooting of both in originally apocalyptic ideas.

Since the nineteenth century, these sketches of history, which are marked by optimism and the belief in progress, have undergone and are undergoing a characteristic modification. This has come about through Darwin's theories of development in the field of the natural sciences and through the enormous advances made by modern technology. The inclusion of the whole of nature in eschatology which could refer to the figurative language of apocalyptic had its way paved already with Oetinger and in Schelling's philosophy of nature, but also in many figures of the Enlightenment (Descartes), and the connection of the hope of the kingdom of God with technical utopias is found ever since the Renaissance. Darwin's teaching about the evolution of the species as well as the belief in technical progress then led, in the nineteenth century, on the one hand to purely secular hopes of the "superman" and the perfect society set free from material pressures. They led, on the other hand, to theological attempts to combine the evolutionary conceptions of the natural sciences with the traditional eschatology. Here we should mention, for example, the Scot James McCosh (died 1894), the Unitarian Minot J.

Savage (died 1918), and the English theologian Henry Drummond (died 1897), for whom God is revealed in natural evolution, which leads to a "more godlike" man. In Drummond's comparison of evolution in the process of creation to a column which is completed with a capital, he understands Christian salvation-history as the pinnacle of universal evolution.

In the twentieth century, the German philosopher Leopold Ziegler and the French Jesuit and anthropologist Teilhard de Chardin, among others, pursue lines of thought in the same direction. The latter connects the Christian "God from above" with the "God advancing." His thought has not only drawn much attention in the Christian realm, but also is playing a large role in the Christian-Marxist dialogue whenever the revolutionary Marxist passion is modified by evolutionary thought.

If such outlines are supported throughout by a progress-oriented optimism, still we are also experiencing today how precisely the advancing insight into the technical process as such and into the social constraints that are connected with it leads to the sketching of counter-utopias. These portray the self-destructive process of the course of this world in thoroughly apocalyptic colors, though without the hope of the dawning of a new eon to follow.

Let us summarize:

The Enlightenment, the Romantic, the early socialist, the idealist, and the naturalist conceptions of the kingdom of God abandon the idea of the sudden upheaval of cosmic conditions through God's intervention, replacing it with the idea of development. Moreover, for the most part, the interest in a definitive goal of history in general disappears. It is dispelled by the construction of a course of history which is constantly and continually striving toward its pinnacle. The divine is at work *in* this advancing historical development as spirit, or reason, or nature.

The theology of the nineteenth century, from Schleiermacher down to the so-called liberals, also shows itself to be influenced in great measure by such currents. At least, the idea of development exerts a great influence. Richard Rothe was able to anticipate the Christian state, the *civitas Dei,* as the perfected form of the kingdom of God. For Albrecht Ritschl, the kingdom of God, whose perfection, to be sure, was remote, was actualized in the expanding community of those who act ethically out of love for their neighbors. In all the utterly nonapocalyptic historical optimism there is maintained, after all, the conception, in essence developed in apocalyptic, of a totality of history which is directed toward a goal.

It may be remarked in passing that in the pernicious proclamation of the "Third Reich," which was to last a thousand years and bring world dominion to the Nordic-Germanic man, apocalyptic expectations survive in totally secularized form. But furthermore, such concepts as "Third Reich" and "Führer" may demonstrably be traced, by way of various intervening links, to the speculation of Joachim of Floris which was kept alive by Lessing, Schelling, and others, and thus ultimately to the apocalyptic outline of history.

To be sure, seen as a whole, apocalyptic motifs exert a much stronger and more original effect in internationalist-universalist Marxism than in the nationalist ideologies of modern times.

For Hegel, the divine spirit and historical reality are ultimately reconciled with each other, and in the nonidealistic optimistic outlines of history, history itself is regarded for the most part as being in principle beneficent. The young Marx, on the other hand, as a critical pupil of Hegel, to a much stronger degree than his teacher adopts apocalyptic conceptions, indeed, essential features of the apocalyptic view of existence itself. In so doing, he refers to the dualistic conception of apocalyptic, insofar as he is able to do so in the light of his atheistic point of departure. It is *not* possible for him to reject history in general in favor of a new eon that will come from God. But Marx in his own way actualizes the idea of the dominion of evil in history, of the ultimate victory of the good, and of the imminent inbreaking of the messianic kingdom at the end of history.

In doing this, Marx must, of course, radically secularize apocalyptic, and in place of the action of God must put the action of men, and in place of waiting on the eschatological upheaval must put revolutionary action—a development which resembles that process in the early period of apocalyptic when alongside the quietistic apocalyptists there appeared the revolutionary Maccabeans and the activistic Zealots. Since Marxism does not abandon the idea of a predetermined and calculable process in history, there arises in that connection the discrepancy, already noted by the early "revisionists," between confidence in the (immanent) laws of history and the urgency of seeking historical change. Marx himself occupies the position of the apocalyptist. His missionary consciousness has a prophetic format, his vision of history the character of revelation, which, to be sure, in harmony with the secular point of view, is worked out as a science.

According to Marx, the driving force in history is the productive process with its various economic opposites, which lead to the formation of the social classes of the bourgeoisie and the proletariat, the "haves" and the "have-nots," the progressives and the reactionaries, the orthodox and the revisionists, the "righteous" and the "sinners." The class struggle necessarily arises out of these contrasts.

History up to this point is judged pessimistically; it is subject to total criticism. It is governed by the typically apocalyptic law of inevitable decay. For, by virtue of the involuntary apportionment of labor through men's own doing, this history has led to a world that has outgrown human control, to the "fallen" world. Thereby man himself also has fallen into "estrangement"; he has lost his "divine image," his true humanness. The course of history must be regarded as a catastrophe.

Apocalyptic stresses the basic contradiction of the old eon in the fact that it was necessary for the world to understand itself as creation in order to have life in it, but instead of this it turned away from the Creator and thus found death. In place of this, Marxism sees the basic contradiction, which determines the evil character of this eon, in economic terms, between capital and labor, exploiters and proletariat.

The "original sin" of the present world-age is the exploitation of men by men; the characteristic mark of the new world is freedom from all compulsion, the satisfying of every need, the end of all relationships of domination and submission. The present age, however, is the time of the upheaval, in which the reddening of the morning sky of the new eon is displayed. The mythical battle between Christ with his angels and the Antichrist with his hosts has already begun historically in the conflict between proletariat and capitalists. It is bound to end in victory for the good; for the Marxist picture of history is just as deterministic as the apocalyptic one, and the dialectic of the economic process allows the totality of history to be surveyed and calculated, so that the revisionist Bernstein could call Karl Marx a Calvinist without God.

In place of the apocalyptic representation of the historical epochs, there appears in Marx the enumeration of various forms of society which are determined by the relationship of the productive forces and the conditions of production.[5] To be sure, "Even when a society has discovered the natural law that governs its course . . . , it can neither bypass nor nullify by decree the natural phases of development. But it can shorten and alleviate the birthpangs," writes Marx in apocalyptic language in the foreword to the first volume of *Das Kapital.* Hence it is not necessary for the working class to actualize ideals; "it has only to liberate the elements of the new society which have already been developed in the womb of the disintegrating bourgeois society."[6] *Because* the end is now coming with such urgency, one can hasten the revolutionary process, a task which in apocalyptic thought God assumes for the protection of his pious ones, by "shortening the days." As in apocalyptic, "knowledge" of the necessary course of history, which allows such interventions which advance the course of revolutionary developments, is possessed by a group of elect ones whose eyes are opened, in one case by God, and in the other by history itself. They gather around them the righteous ones, the proletariat, the avant-garde of the new world, and, as in apocalyptic, those for whom this world is present will soon no longer be obliged to ask, "Why do we not have this our world in our possession?" (4 Esdras 6:59).

Now the time is immediately at hand when the victorious class will establish the classless society. It will renew and redeem the world. The expulsion from Paradise is reversed; creation and man rediscover their harmony: The perfect society "is the perfected unity of essence of man with nature, the true resurrection of nature, the fully achieved naturalism of man and the fully achieved humanism of nature."[7] The "elect" proletariat understand the signs of the times and, now that "the time is fulfilled," will fully bring about the revolutionary change. The concept "revolution," formerly an expression for political upheavals in general, acquires, with Marx, an explicitly eschatological significance and denotes the *one* radical upheaval leading from the old to the new eon.

The "prehistory" of the world now changes into history, the kingdom of compulsion is replaced by the kingdom of liberty, and the kingdom of God without God dawns. The real Genesis occurs at the end, whereby "eternity" is introduced. The fable becomes actuality, and the dream of the Golden Age becomes reality. Desire is matched by actuality, for needs and provisions correspond to each other. The real creation of the world—the creation of the true world, the new eon—is still ahead, but it is just ahead; man is its creator. Therewith man is simultaneously restored to himself and brought back from the estrangement into which the religious distortion of the truth and the economic perversion of reality have sent him.

Then work will be done for satisfaction, because "the society regulates general production and precisely thereby makes it possible for me to do this today, and something else tomorrow, to hunt in the morning, to fish in the afternoon, and to raise cattle in the evening. . . ."[8] All relationships based on domination will come to an end only when the conditions of production are communistically ordered; for even though Marx vigorously contradicted the anarchists of his time because rule can be abolished only by the way prescribed by history, the dictatorship of the proletariat, even in his opinion nothing but an anarchist society is to be the goal of this dictatorship. The state will wither away when there is no longer anything to oppress and subjugate. The rule of men over men and the rule of God, both of them products of perverted economic circumstances, are dissolved at one and the same time by the eternal kingdom of autonomous, happy men.

The Marxist utopia of the new world is described in the apocalyptic writings just as exactly as is the society of exploitation at the end of the old course of the world, the "prehistory":

> The beginning of troubles in every case is a lack of understanding and greed.
> For there arises the striving after deceitful gold and silver. . . . .
>
> It is the source of godlessness and the signpost to disorder,
> Cause of all wars, hateful enemy of peace,
> It makes the children hate their parents and the parents their children.

Without gold a marriage is never held in honor.
And boundaries are set for the land, and guardians over
    every sea,
Craftily apportioned only to those who possess gold and
    treasures.
And as though they should eternally possess the fruitful
    earth,
They exploit the poor, so that they themselves may se-
    cure still
More land for themselves and ostentatiously subject it to
    themselves in greed.
And if the great earth did not have its place so far from
    the starry heavens,
Mankind would not share in the light,
Truly the market would be accessible only to the wealthy,
And the Lord God would have to create another world for
    the beggar.[9]

But as for the new world,

The earth is for all alike, and is not divided by walls and
    boundaries,
But it will bring forth much more fruit
Entirely of itself: life will be shared by all in wealth
    without overlords.
Neither slaves nor masters will be there, neither lofty nor
    lowly ones,
Neither kings nor princes, and all are equal. . . .
[People] will not be concerned about spring and autumn,
    nor about summer and winter,
Nor about marriage and death, nor about buying and
    selling.[10]

Now existence is shared by all, and so is wealth.
The earth is for all alike. . . .[11]

No orators skilled in law, nor a corrupt ruler,
Who sits in judgment. . . .[12]

The health will be distilled in the dew, and sickness will be removed. And trouble and woe and laments will pass away from among men, and joy will walk the whole earth, and no one will die before his time, and nothing untoward will suddenly happen. And trials and accusations and controversies and deeds of revenge and envy and jealousy and hatred and all such will fall under condemnation, and will be uprooted. . . . And in those days the harvesters will not grow weary and those who build will not falter in their work. For the labors will progress by themselves, together with those who work on them in much peace.[13]

. . . because of the infinitely abundant yields, no one at all will be anxious about the stores and provisions already laid up; they will be left to unrestricted use by everyone as he will, without any need first to guard and protect them.[14]

It is unnecessary to show in detail how these pictures of the hope anticipate the Marxist expectation of the classless society in which private ownership of the means of production is abolished, evil will disappear, discriminatory application of justice will cease, the powers of production will grow inexhaustibly, everyone will receive according to his need, work will become play, and a rule of men over men will no longer exist. It was not accidental that Marx called religion, as he understood it, the *imaginative* realization of the human nature and wanted to replace it, adopting its humane intentions, with a *realistic* realization of the human nature; that is to say, with an economic one.

The parallelism of the expectation, however, shows that the Marxist understanding of existence tends toward the same loss of a sense of history as that which characterizes apocalyptic; for even though the classless society, in contradistinction to the thought of apocalyptic, *comes historically*, it stands in fact outside history and no longer knows any conflict, any decision, any progress, or any regression; it possesses no future, but is a timeless present.

Of course, history will go on, and men will also continue to participate in it. Productive powers also will continue to increase; but the equalization, necessitated thereby, of the circumstances of production with the powers of production will progress as of its own accord, without conflict. The turning point between the eons lies behind the world. Man no longer has himself in prospect as possibility, but lives in an inalienable identity in a realm of freedom for which not only the conflicts over freedom but also freedom itself as historical possibility must necessarily be lost.

One final historical effort of man, which surpasses all previous efforts and replaces the divine intervention which is anticipated in apocalyptic, is supposed to bring in the longed-for new eon. This eon will reward such effort with the consummation of history and at the same time with the end of genuine historical possibilities, because history is fulfilled. According to the words of the young Marx, communism is "the solved riddle of history and knows itself to be this solution."[15]

It is not by chance that Ernst Bloch, who adopts the Marxist expectation of the future with a religious emphasis, who sets man on God's throne, and who understands the Marxist "principle of hope" as the true meaning of Jewish-Christian eschatology, corrects popular Marxism at this point. He declares that to the Marxist reality is disclosed as the reality of the *horizon*, the ultimate goal as a whole is still hidden, every goal in turn becomes a means to serve the ultimate goal which in and of itself is still not accessible, and that at the goal there stands what no eye ever yet has seen, the lifting of our *incognito*, the *homo absconditus.*[16] But his making this declaration obviously signifies an effort to cling to the historicality of human existence, at least for the new era of the world which is being actualized.

Even among the "Frankfurt school"—especially by Herbert Marcuse—in opposition to the all too positive affirmations of the future society there can be emphasis on the "power of the negative," with the assurance that we shall come soon enough to the positive. The large-scale rejection of the existing state of things, the active negation of the world as it is, thus tends to suppress—as in so many places in apocalyptic—the glad and hopeful look toward the joy of the new eon. Here, as there, in the background of this "negative dialectic" there obviously stands the phenomenon of the "delay in the Parousia." Instead of the classless society came the dogmas, the disputes over doctrine, and the party apparatus, the Communist "church." At the end of his life, in the foreword to his *Klassenkämpfe* [Struggles of the classes], Friedrich Engels had already admitted this fact of the postponement, to be sure without drawing from it the inescapable consequences.

Apocalyptic is matched, moreover, by the universalistic character of Marxist internationalism, with which, of course, apocalyptic individualism is not related. For the latter is grounded in the necessity of decision against evil which must be made by every individual person. Marx, on the other hand, quite idealistically reckons with the good man and believes that the *humanum*, what is truly human, is only covered over by the social processes, and that it thus will emerge of its own accord through the objective transformation of economic conditions. The "new man" is the latent true man. In other words: It is here, in anthropology, in the understanding of man as sinner, that the apocalyptic and the Marxist understanding of existence first come to a parting of the ways—a necessary difference, when Marx clings to the apocalyptic hope without hope in God. But it is with this difference, too, that the Jewish and Christian criticism of Marxism must begin; for as surely as the apocalyptic way of understanding reality differs essentially from the Jewish faith as well as from the Christian, these three religious currents are bound together by the same biblical image of man: man *is* sinner. That is, evil pertains to man himself. Therefore he is unable to free himself from his state of subjection to evil. Hence he also can never do God's work and bring in the new eon. Man is not-God, he will never become God, and he can never represent God. Therefore too he can experience his freedom only as a continuing liberation; that is to say, only historically. Hence those theological movements of our day which are more or less heavily influenced by Marxism must demonstrate their Christian character primarily in consistently maintaining this biblical image of man. This holds true, for example, for the "theology of hope" of Jürgen Moltmann, for the "theology of revolution" in its various forms, and for all the attempts of a so-called "theology after the death of God," most of which regard the hope for social justice as the only meaningful form of eschatological expectation.

With this we conclude our survey of the aftereffects of

apocalyptic. We cannot do so, however, without remarking that apocalyptic has hardly ever been so influential as it is today, where in its Marxist metamorphosis it exerts a great fascination, not so much upon the proletariat indeed, as Marx hoped, but upon many intellectuals and particularly upon the youth of the time. The latter frequently objectify their own conflict over authority into the Marxist ideology of a society free from any ruling class, instead of overcoming that conflict by means of an active discovery of their own identity; but in this process they do catch sight of the elements of truth in the Marxist analysis of society within the world society of our day. When a preference is shown for the term "late capitalism," this concept is being employed in a thoroughly apocalyptic manner; for the description "late" does not have primary reference to a development which is to be observed in capitalism itself, but to the twilight of the world in general, in which, according to the Marxist interpretation, capitalism necessarily will be replaced by the "new eon."

Leszek Kolakowski concludes his essay "Der revolutionäre Geist" [The revolutionary spirit], in which he makes a comparative analysis of apocalyptic piety and Marxism, with these sentences:

> The idea that the existing world is so utterly corrupt that any improvement of it is inconceivable, and that *precisely for this reason* the world that will succeed it will be the fulness of perfection and the ultimate liberation—this is one of the most monstrous delusions of the human mind. The healthy reason rather suggests to us that, the more corrupt the existing world is shown to be, the longer, more difficult, and uncertain is the way into the dreamed-of kingdom of perfection.

The delusion of which I speak indeed is not an invention of our time. But it must be conceded that it is much less abhorrent to us in religious thinking than in the secular doctrines which assure us that we are in a position to move with a single leap from the abyss of hell to the pinnacle of heaven. *Such* a revolution will never come.

To be sure, Ernst Bloch[17] has used biting irony to attack those who announce a kind of charge of plagiarism against Marx, accuse him of aping mythical originals, and pursue "genealogical research for the mythological grandmother." Now anyone who occupies himself with the phenomenon of "apocalyptic" cannot help inquiring about its historical aftereffects; for the history of apocalyptic ideas belongs to apocalyptic itself just as smoke belongs to fire. Evaluation is not necessarily bound up with such an analysis of intellectual history, and what Marx says is rendered neither more nor less true by the demonstration of analogies or sources in intellectual history, even if, as the quotation from Kolakowski shows, such a comparison evokes the question of truth.

With Marx, as with the other heirs of apocalyptic thought, we can leave open the question to what extent the apocalyptic tradition itself has had a direct or an indirect influence. If it should be established in an individual case that the substantive agreement is not grounded in historical continuity, it would only be all the more clearly demonstrated that apocalyptic does not represent an accidental historical phenomenon, but a possibility of understanding existence which is potential for any time, and therefore is inalienable—a historical possibility even when it hopes for a historical impossibility, the end of history.

NOTES

THE THOUGHT-WORLD OF APOCALYPTIC

1. 4 Esdras 8:52-54; cf. 14:5-8, 45-47; Ethiopic Enoch 42; 82:1.
2. Daniel 11:31; 12:11.
3. Thus in the Ethiopic Book of Enoch especially, the historical revelations are intertwined with the presentation of astronomical and cosmological secrets; the latter have no value of their own, but are meant to underscore the reliability of the historical picture. On this point one may read, for example, Eth. En. 41:3-9.
4. Slavonic Enoch 66:6; cf. 4 Esdras 4:27; 7:12.
5. Pseudo-Clementine Homilies 20:2.
6. Slav. En. 65:7.
7. Syriac Baruch 44:9.
8. Eth. En. 91:17.
9. Eth. En. 51:4-5.
10. Berachoth 17 a; cf. Mark 12:25.
11. 4 Esdras 7:13.
12. Syr. Bar. 85:10.
13. 4 Esdras 14:10.
14. 4 Esdras 5:50-55.
15. 4 Esdras 5:8; 6:21.
16. Jubilees 23:25; Sibylline Oracles II. 154-55.
17. Sib. Or. III. 538; 633; Apocalypse of Abraham 29-30.
18. Sib. Or. II. 164-65.
19. 4 Esdras 6:22.
20. Eth. En. 99:5; Syr. Bar. 27; Apoc. Abr. 30.
21. Sib. Or. III. 539; Eth. En. 80:2; 100:11; Jub. 23:18; Syr. Bar. 27:6.
22. 4 Esdras 6:24.
23. 4 Esdras 5:6.
24. 4 Esdras 5:8.
25. 4 Esdras 5:4.
26. Eth. En. 80:4-7; 4 Esdras 5:5.

27. Sib. Or. III. 796-806.
28. 4 Esdras 5:5.
29. Syr. Bar. 32:1; 4 Esdras 6:16.
30. Syr. Bar. 70:5.
31. 4 Esdras 5:9.
32. Eth. En. 99:4; 100:2; Sib. Or. III. 633, 647; Syr. Bar. 48:32, 35; 70:3.
33. Eth. En. 99:5; 100:1-2; Jub. 23:59; 4 Esdras 5:9; 6:24; Syr. Bar. 70:6.
34. Syr. Bar. 20:1.
35. 4 Esdras 7:32.
36. 4 Esdras 5:42.
37. Eth. En. 100:5 (cf. 96:2).
38. 4 Esdras 7:30-31.
39. 4 Esdras 8:1.
40. Psalm of Solomon 17:44; 18:6.
41. How things will take place at the resurrection is explicitly portrayed, for example, in Syr. Bar. 50–51.

THE ESSENCE OF APOCALYPTIC

1. Eth. En. 2:1–5:3.
2. 1:1-9 and 5:4 ff.
3. Apoc. Abr. 26:5.
4. 4 Esdras 4:47-50.
5. 4 Esdras 4:26.
6. For example, Sanhedrin 97 b.
7. *Ibid.*
8. Syr. Bar. 17.
9. Apoc. Abr. 23:8-9.
10. When Jürgen Moltmann (*Theology of Hope*, p. 137) speaks of a "historifying of the world" by apocalyptic, he would be correct if thereby he meant that in apocalyptic, as distinct from Greek thought, the whole of the reality of the world is interpreted historically. But since he speaks of the apocalyptic "historifying of the world in the category of the universal eschatological future," he is incorrect. For the apocalyptist confronts this historical world with radical pessimism. For him it has no future at all; its "eschaton" is the universal collapse. It is only the new world that permits hope, a world which God will create without any continuity with the old, and which for the apocalyptist no longer possesses any genuine historical dimensions.
11. 4 Esdras 7:116 ff.

12. Syr. Bar. 48:42.
13. Syr. Bar. 54:19.
14. 4 Esdras 8:47.
15. 4 Esdras 9:22.
16. 4 Esdras 9:14.
17. Eth. En. 98:4-5.
18. Eth. En. 103:9 ff.
19. Eth. En. 46:8; 53:5 ff.
20. 4 Esdras 8:56 ff.; cf. 7:23-24; 7:79.
21. D. Rössler, *Gesetz und Geschichte*, 1960.
22. 4 Esdras 10:16.
23. 4 Esdras 14:21.
24. For example, Syr. Bar. 46:4 ff.; 48:24; 51:3 ff.
25. Syr. Bar. 48:40, 47; 54:14.

THE HISTORY OF THE STUDY OF APOCALYPTIC

1. Adolf Hilgenfeld, *Die jüdische Apokalyptik in ihrer geschichtlichen Entwicklung* (1857), p. 1.
2. *Ibid.*, p.viii.
3. *Ibid.*, p. 2.
4. *Ibid.*, p. 8.
5. *Ibid.*, p. 9.
6. *Ibid.*, pp. 10-11.
7. *Ibid.*, p. 15.
8. *Ibid.*, p. 16.
9. Hugo Gressmann, *Ursprung der israelitisch-jüdischen Eschatologie* (1905), p. 158.
10. Wilhelm Bousset, *Die Religion des Judentums im späthellenistischen Zeitalter* (1903; 4th ed., 1966), p. 524.
11. *Ibid.*, p. 213.
12. *Ibid.*, p. 211.
13. *Ibid.*, p. 213.
14. *Ibid.*, p. 212.
15. Rudolf Otto, *The Kingdom of God and the Son of Man: A Study in the History of Religion* (1933; 2d ed., 1940; English trans., 1943, from the rev. German ed., by Floyd V. Filson and Bertram Lee Woolf), p. 48 n. 1.
16. *Ibid.*, pp. 41-42.
17. *Ibid.*, p. 49.
18. *Ibid.*, p. 59.
19. Karl Barth, *The Epistle to the Romans* (1922; English trans., 1933, from the 6th German ed., by Edwyn C. Hoskyns), p. 314.

20. H. H. Rowley, *The Relevance of Apocalyptic* (new and rev. ed., 1963), pp. 181-82.
21. Ernst Käsemann, *New Testament Questions of Today* (1969; trans. W. J. Montague), pp. 109-10.

APOCALYPTIC AND THE OLD TESTAMENT

1. Syr. Bar. 10:3.
2. H. D. Preuss, *Jahweglaube und Zukunftserwartung*, p. 212.
3. *Ibid.*, p. 213.
4. Gerhard von Rad, *Old Testament Theology* (1965; trans. D. M. Stalker), II, 303-4.
5. Rowley, *Relevance of Apocalyptic*, p. 168.
6. Cf. also 4 Esdras 12:34; Syr. Bar. 40:1-4; Eth. En. 91:11-13.
7. Eth. En. 81:7-8.
8. Eth. En. 94:2-3.

APOCALYPTIC AND GNOSIS

1. As cited in Otto, *Kingdom of God and the Son of Man*, p. 15.
2. Eth. En. 6–8; 15:8–16:1.
3. Syr. Bar. 23:4.
4. 4 Esdras 4:35.
5. 4 Esdras 7:116 ff.
6. Syr. Bar. 54:19.
7. 4 Esdras 7:11-12.
8. Syr. Bar. 66:3.
9. 4 Esdras 8:3; 8:1.

THE ORIGIN OF APOCALYPTIC: RELIGIOHISTORICAL CONNECTIONS

1. Sib. Or. II. 196 ff.; cf. IV. 173 ff.
2. Bundahisn 34.
3. Isaiah 45:1 ff.; 46:11 ff.; 48:12 ff.
4. Eduard Meyer, *Ursprung und Anfänge des Christentums*, II, 64.
5. 4 Esdras 4:12.
6. Wilhelm Bousset, *op. cit.*, p. 510.
7. Cf. R. M. Grant, *Gnosticism and Early Christianity*, 1959, pp. 27 ff.

THE ORIGIN OF THE APOCALYPTIC MOVEMENT IN JUDAISM

1. Gerhard von Rad, *Theologie des Alten Testaments*, II (4th ed., 1965), 320. (Translator's note: The English translation of this

Notes

work, cited above, was made from an earlier edition of the book,
and this passage does not appear there.)

2. Philipp Vielhauer, introduction to "Apocalypses and Related Subjects," in Edgar Hennecke–Wilhelm Schneemelcher, *New Testament Apocrypha* (English trans., 1965, by R. McL. Wilson), II, 598.
3. Gerhard von Rad, *Old Testament Theology*, II, 117.
4. Otto Plöger, *Theocracy and Eschatology* (trans. S. Rudman), 1968.
5. *Ibid.*, pp. 43-44.
6. *Ibid.*, p. 46.
7. *Ibid.*, p. 108.
8. *Ibid.*, p. 49.
9. *Ibid.*, p. 50.
10. H. Ringgren, in *Die Religion in Geschichte und Gegenwart*, 3d ed., Vol. I, col. 464.
11. W. Foerster, *Neutestamentliche Zeitgeschichte*, 2d ed., 1955, I, 52.
12. Bousset, *op. cit.*, p. 472.
13. Cf., for example, Jer. 22:13; Ps. 49:7; Prov. 11:28.
14. Eth. En. 103:14-15.
15. Sib. Or. VIII. 24 ff.
16. Thus Hans G. Kippenburg, in *Numen*, 17 (1970), 211 ff.
17. Otto, *op. cit.*, pp. 41-42.

APOCALYPTIC AND CHRISTIANITY

1. Hilgenfeld, *op. cit.*, p. 2.
2. Schweitzer's book appeared in 1906.
3. Ernst Käsemann, "The Beginnings of Christian Theology," in *New Testament Questions of Today*, pp. 81-107.
4. Ernst Käsemann, "On the Subject of Primitive Christian Apocalyptic," in *New Testament Questions of Today*, pp. 108-137. The quotations are from pp. 113 and 112, respectively.
5. 1 Cor. 15:12-57; 1 Thess. 4:13-18; 2 Thess. 2:3-12.

MESSIAH AND SON OF MAN

1. Syr. Bar. 29:3*b*-8 (Charles). Similar utopian portrayals of the messianic age are found in Syr. Bar. 36 ff. and 70 ff., as well as in Sib. Or. III. 741 ff., 777 ff.
2. Syr. Bar. 74:2, 3*b* (Charles).
3. Jub. 37:21-22.
4. Syr. Bar. 40:1-2 (Charles).

The Apocalyptic Movement

5. 4 Esdras 7:26-31 (Charles).
6. Cf. Sib. Or. III. 743, 756-57.
7. Eth. En. 46:1-4 (Charles).
8. Eth. En. 62:13-16a (Charles). One may compare further Eth. En. 38:2; 39:6-7; 48:4 ff.; 55:4; and 69:27 ff., as well as Mark 13:24-27, an apocalyptic text without visible Christian revision.
9. Bousset, *op. cit.*, p. 267.

THE APOCALYPTIC LITERATURE

1. Testament of Levi 18.
2. Hilgenfeld, *op. cit.*, p. 16.
3. Readily accessible, for example, in *The Dead Sea Scriptures*, ed. Theodore H. Gaster.
4. Cf. 1 Cor. 2:6-8; Luke 4:6; Rev. 12:9; John 12:31.
5. Dan. 2:44; 3:33; 7:13 ff.
6. 2 Cor. 4:4; John 12:31; 14:30; 16:11; cf. 1 Cor. 2:6, 8; Luke 4:6.

THE HISTORICAL EFFECTS OF APOCALYPTIC

1. Above, pp. 206ff.
2. Sib. Or. VIII. 37 ff.
3. E. Benz, *Ecclesia Spiritualis*, 1934, p. 50.
4. William Godwin, "On Property," in *Enquiry Concerning Political Justice* (1796), II, 385.
5. Cf. the preface to the *Critique of Political Economy*.
6. *The Civil War in France*, Part III.
7. *Pariser Manuskripte*, R. K. 209/210, p. 77.
8. *Deutsche Ideologie*, Kröners Taschenausgabe 209, p. 361.
9. Sib. Or. VIII. 17 ff.
10. Sib. Or. II. 319 ff.
11. Sib. Or. VIII. 208-9.
12. Sib. Or. VIII. 112-13.
13. Syr. Bar. 73-74.
14. Philo, *De praemiis* 103.
15. *Pariser Manuskripte*, R. K. 209/210, p. 76.
16. Ernst Bloch, *Das Prinzip Hoffnung*, p. 1628 *et passim*.
17. *Ibid.*, pp. 1611-12.

BIBLIOGRAPHY

Bate, H. N. *The Sibylline Oracles, Books III-V*. London, 1918.
Box, G. H. *The Apocalypse of Abraham and the Ascension of Isaiah*. London, 1918.
———. *The Ezra-Apocalypse*. London, 1912.
Charles, R. H. *The Apocrypha and Pseudepigrapha of the Old Testament*. 2 vols. Oxford, 1912.
———. *The Book of Enoch*. Oxford, 1912.
———. *The Book of Jubilees*. London, 1902.
———. *The Testaments of the Twelve Patriarchs*. London, 1908.
Harris, J. Rendel, and Mingana, A. *The Odes and Psalms of Solomon*. 2 vols. Manchester, 1916, 1920.
Hennecke, Edgar. *The New Testament Apocrypha*. Third edition, edited by Wilhelm Schneemelcher. 2 vols. English translation edited by R. McL. Wilson. Philadelphia, 1963, 1965.
Koch, Klaus. *The Rediscovery of Apocalyptic*. Translated by Margaret Kohl. Naperville, Ill., 1972.
Otto, Rudolf. *The Kingdom of God and the Son of Man*. Translated by Floyd V. Filson and Bertram Lee-Woolf. London, 1943.
Plöger, Otto. *Theocracy and Eschatology*. Translated by S. Rudman. Oxford, 1968.
Oesterley, W. O. E. *II Esdras (The Ezra Apocalypse)*. London, 1933.
Rad, Gerhard von. *Old Testament Theology*. Translated by D. M. Stalker. 2 vols. Edinburgh, 1962, 1965.
Rowley, H. H. *The Relevance of Apocalyptic*. Revised edition. New York, 1963.
Russell, D. S. *The Method and Message of Jewish Apocalyptic*. Philadelphia, 1964.